"This is the best movie about kids in small-town America since *Red Sky at Morning* and an absolute must for anyone who has as much nostalgia about growing up in the late 1950s and early 1960s as I do. This is the story of all our lives, and it is magnificently acted and edited and directed and photographed and scored, and it introduces a host of marvelous young actors to the screen as real as the fading photos in a high school yearbook. A breathless cat's meow of a movie with enough energy and talent to get the next man to the moon and back!"   —Rex Reed

"A jumping entertainment that keeps you hip-deep in memory and reminiscence."
                              —Archer Winsten, *The New York Post*

"This movie is a beauty. Funny and touching!"
                              —Gene Shalit, NBC-TV

"Brilliant . . . bittersweet. . . . Lucas and his co-writers, Gloria Katz and William Huyck, build a structure of rich comic incident that is rooted in wisdom about adolescence. . . . Lucas has captured a moment recognizable to every generation, when all of us were shoring up our sapling egos with the roles and defenses we would need in the years ahead."
—Paul D. Zimmerman, *Newsweek*

"Sharp and tender, funny and sad, gritty and moving. In a word, *American Graffiti* is beautiful!"   —Stuart Klein, WNEW-TV

"This superb and singular film catches not only the charm and tribal energy of the teen-age 1950s, but also the listlessness and the resignation that underscored it all like an incessant bass line in one of the rock-'n'-roll songs of the period. Few films have shown quite so well the eagerness, the sadness, the ambition, and small defeats of a generation of young Americans. Bitchin', as they said back then. Superfine!"—Jay Cocks, *Time Magazine*

AMERICAN GRAFFITI

A SCREENPLAY BY
GEORGE LUCAS,
GLORIA KATZ, AND WILLARD HUYCK

BALLANTINE BOOKS • NEW YORK

Library of Congress Catalog Card Number: 73-17640

SBN 345-23690-4-150

This edition published by arrangement with Grove Press

First Printing: December, 1973

Design by Steve Heller

Printed in the United States of America

BALLANTINE BOOKS, INC.
201 East 50th Street, New York, N.Y. 10022

AMERICAN GRAFFITI

RADIO

On a dark screen an immense amber light appears and an electric humming begins. The eerie light glows brighter and illuminates a single huge number—11. We hear static and a large vertical band of red floats mysteriously across the screen.

Pulling back slowly, we watch the glowing band traverse back and forth over the amber light and past more numbers appearing—70 . . . 90 . . . 110 . . . 130. And we begin to hear voices—strange songs, fading conversations and snatches of music drifting with static.

Pulling back further, we realize it is a car radio filling the screen and radio stations we're hearing, until the indicator stops. There's a pause . . . and suddenly we are hit by a blasting-out-of-the-past, Rocking and Rolling, turn-up-the-volume, pounding Intro to a Vintage 1962 Golden Week-End Radio Show—back when things were simpler and the music was better.

And now a wolf howl shatters through time as the legendary Wolfman Jack hits the airwaves, his gravel voice shrieking and growling while the music pumps and grinds. . . .

WOLFMAN: Awwrigght, baay-haay-baay! I got a oldie for ya—gonna knock ya right on de flowa—baay-haay-hee-baay!

The Wolfman howls like a soulful banshee as "Rock Around the Clock" blasts forth.

MEL'S DRIVE-IN–DUSK

A neon drive-in casts long shadows across a vast parking lot as the sun drops behind a distant hill. A

large neon sign buzzes in the foreground . . . **MEL'S
DRIVE-IN**, *while in the background, "Rock Around
The Clock" blares from the radio of a beautiful decked
and channeled, white with red trim, tuck-and-rolled
'58 Chevy Impala that glides into the drive-in.*

Main titles appear over action.

*Steve Bolander stops the elegant machine and gets
out. He looks around, then walks to the front of the
car and leans against the flame-covered hood. Steve
is eighteen, good-looking in a conservative, button-
down, short-sleeved shirt. Most likely to succeed, president of his graduating class. He looks around the
empty drive-in, then hears a funny little horn.*

*A Vespa scooter bumps into the lot. A young kid
waves at him—and suddenly grabs the handlebars
again as the scooter nearly topples.*

*Terry Fields ("The Toad") maneuvers the scooter
next to Steve's Chevy but misjudges and ricochets off*

the trash can before stopping. Terry grins sheepishly.

He's seventeen, short but plenty loud, both vocally and sartorially in his pink and black shirt, levis, and white bucks. He looks slightly ridiculous but always thinks he's projecting an air of supercool.

Steve watches Terry smooth back his shiny ducktail and primp his waterfall to a perfect cascade over his forehead. He unbuttons his shirt one more button and lowers his pants to look tough.

Terry walks over and leans against the flamed car, imitating Steve who pays him no mind. In the background, we hear the Wolfman howling with the music. The record ends and a barrage of humor begins from Wolfman Jack. The Wolfman is an unseen companion to all the kids. Witty and knowledgeable about the trivia that counts, he's their best friend, confidant, and guardian angel.

Now a grey, insect-like Citroën deux-chevaux putters

into the parking lot and stops on the other side of the
lot. Steve and Terry watch Curt Henderson get out.

Curt stands by his little car. He's seventeen, a curly
bespectacled, scraggly kid with a summer-grown
moustache and a paperback stuck in his bermuda
shorts. Curt thinks of himself as the town cynic. In
reality, he's a hopeless romantic. He starts over to his
buddies.

TERRY: Hey, whadaya say, Curt? Last night in town,
you guys gonna have a little bash before you leave?
STEVE: The Moose have been lookin' for you all day,
man.

Steve reaches into his pocket and hands Curt an
envelope without saying anything. Curt opens it slowly
and pulls out a check.

CURT (*sarcastic*): Oh great . . .

TERRY: Whadaya got, whadaya got? (*snooping over his shoulder*) Wow—two thousand dollars. Two thousand doll——!!

Steve looks at Curt suspiciously; Curt seems somehow guilty.

STEVE: Mr. Jenning couldn't find you, so he gave it to me to give to you. He said he's sorry it's so late, but it's the first scholarship the Moose Lodge has given out. Oh yeah, he says they're all very proud of you.

Curt hands the envelope back to Steve.

CURT: Well . . . ah . . . why don't you hold onto it for a while?

STEVE: What's with you? It's yours! Take it! I don't want it.

TERRY: I'll take it.

CURT: Steve . . . Ah, I think we'd better have a talk. I've gotten——

Suddenly a horn honks and they all turn. Laurie Henderson pulls into the drive-in and waves to them. She is driving the family's '58 Edsel.

STEVE: Your sister calls. I'll talk to you later.

CURT: Now, Steve! Let her wait.

STEVE: Okay, make it short and sweet.

CURT: Yeah, well . . . Listen . . . (*clearing his throat*) I . . . I don't think I'm going tomorrow

STEVE: What! Come on, what are you talking about?

CURT: I don't know. I was thinking I might wait for a year . . . go to city——

8

Laurie honks the horn a couple of times. Steve ignores her. There is a long moment and Curt looks uncomfortable.

STEVE: You chicken fink.

CURT: Wait, let me explain——

STEVE: You can't back out now! After all we went through to get accepted. We're finally getting out of this turkey town and now you want to crawl back into your cell—look, I gotta talk to Laurie (*he hands the check back to Curt*). Now take it. We're leaving in the morning. Okay?

Suddenly, there's an ear-splitting roar and they all turn as a yellow '32 Ford deuce coupe—chopped, lowered and sporting a Hemi-V8—bumps into the lot. The low slung classic rumbles and parks at the rear of the drive in.

Big John Milner, twenty-two, sits in his Ford, tough and indifferent, puffing on a Camel. He wears a white T-shirt and a butch haircut molded on the sides into a ducktail. A cowboy in a deuce coupe—simple, sentimental and cocksure of himself.

STEVE: You wanna end up like John? You can't stay
  seventeen forever.
CURT: I just want some time to think. What's the rush?
  I'll go next year.
STEVE: We'll talk later.

*Steve walks off toward Laurie's Edsel. Laurie gets
out. She's wearing a letterman's sweater with a large
"Class of '62" emblazoned on the shoulder. Steve goes
to her and they hug.*

*On the radio, the music ends, and the Wolfman's
intro tune comes on.*

RADIO (*singing*): "Here comes the Wolfman—Wolfman Jack!"
WOLFMAN (*voice over*): Oh, We're gonna rock and roll
  ourselves to death, baby. You got the Wolfman
  Jack Show!

MEL'S DRIVE-IN—NIGHT

*As the radio blares "Sixteen Candles," we see that
with the darkness Burger City has come alive. A con-
tinual line of hot rods pulls into the parking lot to
check out the parked cars, then returns to the main-
drag. Carhops glide by on roller skates.*

*Curt and John are fooling around in front of the
deuce coupe. A horn honks and they turn as a '60 Ford
with three girls in it slows by them. A girl leans out
the window and smiles.*

GIRL: Hi John!

*The girls in the car all screech and giggle as they
zoom off.*

JOHN: Not too good, huh?

CURT: Why is it every girl that comes around here is ugly? Or has a boyfriend? Where is the dazzling beauty I've been searching for all my life?

John watches the procession of gleaming cars traveling through the hot night.

JOHN: I know what you mean. The pickin's are really gettin' slim. The whole strip is shrinking. Ah, you know, I remember about five years ago, take you a couple of hours and a tank full of gas just to make one circuit. It was really somethin'.

Suddenly, in the distance, there's a blood-curdling scream from an incredible high-performance engine. The entire drive-in stops and listens.

CURT: Hey, John. Someone new in town.

JOHN: Ahhh.

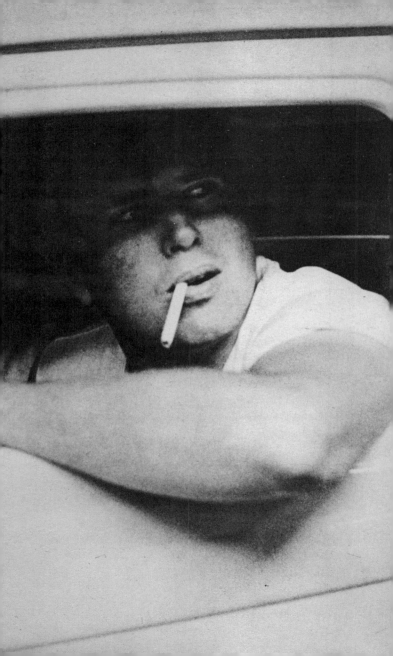

CURT: You gonna go after him?

JOHN: Hey, listen, Professor, if he can't find me, then he ain't even worth racin', right?

CURT: The big shot!

Across the swarming parking lot, Steve sits in the front seat of his chevy with Laurie. Budda Macrae, a car hop, leans down to attach a tray to Steve's window, showing off her tight blouse.

BUDDA: A cherry-vanilla coke and a chocolate mountain. Anything else you want, Steve?

Steve shakes his head.

If there is you let me know now. Just honk and I'm yours.

She tucks in her blouse a little tighter, gives him a hot look and goes to get the other tray. Budda takes the other tray around the car, almost shoves it in the window where Laurie is sitting.

BUDDA: One fries—grab it before I drop it.

She gives Laurie an antagonistic look and goes off. Steve laughs. Laurie smiles. She's seventeen, very pretty, with big doe-eyes, and a short bobbed hairdo. She pushes up the sleeves on Steve's letterman sweater, which is sizes too large for her. His class ring glints on a chain around her neck. Laurie is sweet, the image of vulnerability, but with a practical and self-preserving mind beneath.

STEVE: Where was I?

LAURIE: Um, how you thought high school romances

14

were goofy and we started going together just because you thought I was kinda cute and funny, but then you suddenly realized you were in love with me, it was serious . . . and ah . . . oh, you were leadin' up to somethin' kinda big.

STEVE: You make it sound like I'm giving dictation. Well, seriously, what I meant was, that ah . . . since we do care for each other so much, and since we should really consider ourselves as adults. Now, I, ah . . . could I have a couple of those fries?

Through the windshield of the Chevy, they see Terry run by in front of them, chasing Budda Macrae who's outdistancing him on her roller skates.

TERRY: Come on, Budda. Come on. . . .

Steve watches them go by, then looks back at Laurie.

STEVE: Ah, where was I?

LAURIE: . . . "consider ourselves adults" . . .

Laurie pretends to be interested in her french fries, but is obviously expecting something big.

STEVE: Right . . . right . . . anyway, I thought maybe, before I leave, we could ah . . . agree that . . . that seeing other people while I'm away can't possibly hurt, you know?

Laurie hasn't looked up but her mood has changed like a mask.

LAURIE: You mean dating other people?

STEVE: I think it would strengthen our relationship.

Then we'd know for sure that we're really in love. Not that there's any doubt.

Steve smiles and then looks at her. He stops smiling. They listen to the radio for an awkward moment. Laurie struggles to hold back her tears. With obvious difficulty, she turns to him and smiles. He's expected something different and doesn't know what to do, so he smiles back.

LAURIE: I think you're right. I mean, we're not kids anymore, and it's silly to think that when we're three thousand miles apart we shouldn't be able to see other people and go out.

Laurie takes his ring on the chain from around her neck and puts it in her purse.

STEVE: Laurie, now, listen, I didn't ask for that back. I think that . . .
LAURIE: I know. I just sort of think it's juvenile now. I'll keep it at home. It's less conspicuous there.
STEVE: You don't want to wear it?
LAURIE: I didn't say that. I understand and I'm not upset. I mean, I can't expect you to be a monk or something while you're away.

Steve just looks at her and nods. The Wolfman howls an intro to "Gee" by the Crows.
Outside, skooting around the drive-in after Budda, Terry is pleading with the sexy car hop as she delivers a tray to a car.

TERRY: . . . and I have a really sharp record collection. I even have "Pledging My Love" by Johnny Ace. Anyway, how can you love Nelson when he's going

16

out with Marilyn Gator. Since he dumped on you maybe we could——

BUDDA: He didn't dump on me, you little dip. Hi, Steve!

Her tone changes immediately. Terry looks sour and turns around to Steve who's getting out of the chevy. Budda leaves, wiggling her butt for Steve.

TERRY: She's a little conceited—just playing hard to get.
STEVE: Listen, I came over here to talk to you about——
TERRY: Any time, buddy. I'm your man. Nothing I like better than chewing the rug with a pal. You talk, I'll listen. I'm all ears. Shoot.
STEVE: Shut up.
TERRY: Sure.
STEVE: Terry, I'm going to let you take care of my car while we're away—at least until Christmas. I'm afraid if I leave it with my——

Steve notices Terry isn't with him any more and turns. Terry is standing frozen to a spot.

STEVE: What's wrong?

Terry tries to talk, much like a shell-shocked war veteran. His mouth moves but only a gurgle comes out.
Curt is standing by the Chevy, talking with his sister Laurie. She's still upset by what Steve said to her.

CURT: Hey, sis—what's wrong?

LAURIE: Nothing.

Meanwhile, they watch Terry as Steve explains to him about the car.

STEVE: Now listen, only 30 weight Castrol-R. I've written the tire pressure and stuff on a pad in the glove compartment. Are you listening?

The others are watching now as Terry shakes his head mechanically.

CURT: What's wrong, he's crying!

There is indeed a tear rolling down Terry's cheek.

TERRY: I can't . . . believe . . . it. (*He starts toward the car and gently caresses its paint.*) I don't know what to say. I'll . . . love and protect this car until death do us part. (*He circles the car.*) This is a superfine machine. This may even be better than Daryl Starbird's superfleck moonbird. It *is* better than Daryl Starbird's.

Laurie watches Terry, realizing that like the car, she'll be left behind as a fond memory. She turns and looks at Steve, who's been watching her. There's a moment between them . . .
Budda comes by with an empty tray. Terry sees her and wipes his eyes. He walks up to her, a strange look on his face.

TERRY: Budda, how would you like to go to the drive-in movies with me?

The idea is so preposterous that even Budda is speechless. She looks around at others.

BUDDA: You've got to be kidding!

TERRY: Would I kid you about a thing like that? I want you to know that something has happened to me tonight that is going to change everything. I've got a new . . .

John walks up quietly and casually pulls down hard on the back pockets of Terry's low riding levis. Terry's pants drop around his ankles. There is general hysteria as Terry quickly pulls up his pants.

TERRY: Car!! All right, who's the wise—(*He turns and sees John and changes his tune.*) Oh, John—verrry funny. (*He tries to laugh with the others.*)

JOHN: Hey, did she do that to you?

STEVE: Let's get going. It seems like we've spent most of our lives in this parking lot.

TERRY: Hey, Curt, let's bomb around, I wanna try out my new wheels!

CURT: I'd like to, Toad, but I'm going with Steve and Laurie to the hop. I'd just slow you down anyway.

TERRY: Yeah, tonight things are going to be different.

JOHN: Hey, wait a minute, you're goin' to the Hop? The Freshman Hop?

CURT: Yeah.

JOHN: Oh, come on, man. That place is for kids. You two just got your ass out of there. Don't go back now.

CURT: You ain't got no emotions?

TERRY: We're gonna remember all of the good times, is what we're gonna do.

JOHN: Yeah, well, go.

CURT: Why don't you come with us?

JOHN: Bullshit, man!

CURT: Come on. For old time's sake.

JOHN: Yeah, yeah . . . Well, listen. You go. Go ahead, Curtsy, baby. You go on over there and you remember all the good times you won't be having. I ain't goin' off to some goddamned fancy college. I'm stayin' right here. Havin' fun, as usual.

John walks angrily to his coupe, gets in and slams the door. Curt looks at the others and shrugs.

TERRY: Jesus, Milner, you're in a great mood tonight.

Curt goes over and stands by the window of the yellow coupe.

CURT: What's the matter John? Did I say somethin' wrong? I'm sorry.

JOHN: Ah, man, it's nothin'.

CURT: Well, we'll see you later, okay?

JOHN: Right.

CURT: We'll all do somethin' together. You know, before Steve leaves.

John looks at him suspiciously.

JOHN: Okay, wait a minute. Now, you're not going?

CURT: I don't know.

John shakes his head. On the radio, Wolfman is taking a call from a listener—

MAN (*voice over*): Wolfman?

WOLFMAN (*voice over*): Who is this?

MAN: This is Joe . . . in Little Rock, way down in the Valley.

WOLFMAN: You callin' from Little Rock, California?

MAN: Long distance.

WOLFMAN: My, my, my . . . listen, man, what kind of entertainment you got in that town?

MAN: All we got is you.

John roars his engine and pulls the yellow deuce coupe into a screeching take-off out of the drive-in. Terry and Curt watch him go off.

MAIN STREET, MODESTO—NIGHT

During the day, G street is a line of used car lots, small shops, tacky department stores and greasy spoons. At night, it is transformed into an endless parade of kids in flamed, lowered and customed machines who rumble down the one way street, through the seemingly adultless, heat-drugged little town.

Police cars glide ominously with the flow of traffic. In parked cars, couples neck between flashing headlights. Guys looking cool in a '56 Chevy sit in the slouched position of the true Low Rider—and over it all the music and the Wolfman can be heard. Just now, it's "Runaway" by Del Shannon.

John travels with the flow of traffic, watching some dopey guys shooting squirt guns from a moving car. John drives the deuce coupe effortlessly. He looks over at a car pacing alongside of his own.

JOHN: Hey, Zudo.

A sweaty looking guy turns and nods from the window.

PAZUDO: Hey, Milner.

JOHN: Hey, man, what happened to your flathead?

PAZUDO: Huh?

JOHN: What happened to your flathead?

PAZUDO: Ah, your mother!

JOHN: What?

PAZUDO: Your mother. Hey, we been talkin' about you.

JOHN: Yeah?

PAZUDO: Yeah. There's a very wicked '55 Chevy lookin' for you.

JOHN: Yeah, I know.

PAZUDO: Watch out for the cop that's in Jerry's Cherry.

JOHN: Yeah. All right, thanks.

John nods and the two cars pull apart down the street.

TRAVELING G STREET—STEVE'S WHITE '58 CHEVY

The Rock and Roll blares as Terry the Toad cruises along the main drag, singing along with the music. Sitting low in his seat, he looks around, his face aglow, experiencing a new world from the inside of a really fine car. This is the greatest thing that has happened to Terry in seventeen long years of being a short loser.

Terry turns a corner and another car pulls alongside. A guy looks out the window.

GUY: Hey, Toad.

Terry looks over and smiles coolly, proud of his new wheels.

GUY (*leaning out the window*): Is that you in that beautiful car? (*Terry nods modestly*) Geez, what a waste of machinery.

Terry's smile changes to a scowl as the car pulls away from him. Terry accounts the slight to jealousy. Then he forgets it and enjoys driving the beautiful Chevy again. Another car pulls alongside of him as he cruises along slowly.

GIRL: Hey, kid.

Terry looks over at the car cruising next to him. In the back seat, a guy has dropped his trousers and is pushing his bare buttocks against the side window—a classic BA complete with pressed ham. Terry looks

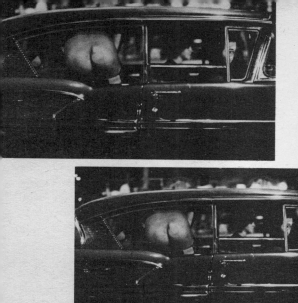
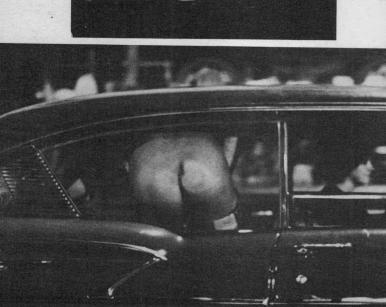

away, wondering why this is still happening to him, even in his new car.

TRAVELING G STREET—LAURIE'S '58 EDSEL

Curt is in the back seat gazing out the window at the dark main street of the small farm community. Steve and Laurie are talking quietly in the front seat. Laurie is sitting near the window and it sounds like Steve is trying to convince her to move over. Laurie finally does. His arm goes around her and her head rests on his shoulder.

Curt is laughing as the Wolfman harasses someone on the radio. The Wolfman is placing a call.

WOLFMAN (*voice over*): Here we go with another call out of the station. Can you dig it? Answer the phone, dummy.

MAN (*voice over*): Pinkie's Pizza.

WOLFMAN: Ah, yeah, listen, you got any more of those secret agent spy-scopes?

MAN: Hit parade on the stethoscope?

WOLFMAN: No. No, the secret agent spy-scope, man. That pulls in the moon, the sky and the planets . . . and the satellites and the little bitty space men.

MAN: You must have the wrong number, partner.

WOLFMAN: 'Bye.

Wolfman cuts into "Why Do Fools Fall in Love." Curt is laughing in the back of the car, as he listens to the ever-present D.J.

Steve slows the Edsel to a stop at the next light. Curt glances over at a classic white '56 Thunderbird and sits up. In the T-bird, a girl watches him. Blonde, beautiful, her hair, backlit by a used car lot, seems to glow, making her look almost ethereal. Curt doesn't move, as if afraid of scaring her away. She smiles faintly—then says something, so softly it's lost...

CURT: What?

Curt struggles to lower his window. She repeats it, but he can't hear. The light changes. She smiles once more and is gone.

CURT (*shouting*): What? What? ! ! !
STEVE: We didn't say anything.
CURT: Quick! Hang a right!
STEVE: What? Why?
CURT: Cut over to G Street, I've just seen a vision! She was a goddess. You've got to catch her!
STEVE: I didn't see anything.
LAURIE: We're not going to spend the night chasing girls for you.
CURT: I'm telling you, this was the most perfect, dazzling creature I've ever seen.
STEVE: She's gone. Forget it.
CURT: She spoke to me. She spoke to me, right through the window. I think she said, "I love you."

Curt looks at his sister and Steve in the front seat. They are bored by his romantic visions.

CURT: That means nothing to you people? You have no romance, no soul? She—someone wants me. Someone roaming the streets wants me! Will you turn the corner?

Laurie looks around at him and seems to pity his flights of poetic fantasy. Curt sits back and shakes his head.

PARKING LOT

Big John sits in his deuce coupe, backed into the parking lot of the Acme Fall-out Shelter Co., the prime spot in town for girl watching. A guy in wrap-around dark glasses leans by the car next to John. They watch a group of laughing girls cruise by in a Studebaker.

JOHN: Oh, oh. Later.
GUY: Alligator.

John turns on his lights and swings the deuce coupe out into the flow of traffic, after the Studebaker.
John accelerates and pulls alongside the Studebaker. The girl in the front seat rolls down her window. John grins and yells over at the carload of cuties.

JOHN: Hey, you're new around here. Where're you from?
FIRST GIRL: Turlock.
JOHN: Turlock? You know a guy named Frank Bartlett?
FIRST GIRL: No. Does he go to Turlock High?
JOHN: Well, he used to. He goes to J.C. now.
FIRST GIRL: Do you go to J.C.?
JOHN: Yeah, sure.
FIRST GIRL: Oh, wow! Do you know Guy Phillips?
JOHN: Yeah, sure. I got him in a class.

FIRST GIRL: He's so boss.

JOHN: How would you like to ride around with me for awhile?

FIRST GIRL: I'm sorry, I can't. I'm going steady.

JOHN: Ah, come on!

FIRST GIRL: I just can't.

JOHN: You're just ridin' around with a bunch of girls. Hey, how about somebody else in there? Anybody else want to go for a ride?

The girls chatter and giggle among themselves. One of the girls dangles a bra out the back window, and they all break into hysterical laughter. The girls try to accelerate ahead, but John stays alongside their car.

JOHN: Aw, come on . . . I got plenty of room. It's dangerous to have that many people in a car. Cops see ya, you're had. You got nothing to fear, I'm as harmless as a baby kitten.

A small voice rises above the chatter.

CAROL: I'll go. I'll go.

FIRST GIRL: Judy's sister wants to ride with you. Is that all right?

JOHN (*grinning*): Yeah, sure, Judy—her sister—her mother—anybody. I'll take 'em all. Listen, we'll go up and stop at that light. It'll turn red by the time we get there. All right?

The first girl grins and nods. John winks at her.

JOHN: You ever get tired of going steady with somebody that ain't around—I'm up for grabs.

The cars stop at the light. A girl rushes out from the

Studey and runs around the back of John's coupe. She opens the door and climbs in fast as the light changes.

The Studebaker pulls off fast. John pushes through the gears and turns and smiles at his pick-up, as "That'll Be the Day" plays on the Wolfman Jack Show.

JOHN: So, you're Judy's little sister.

Carol Morrison shakes her head. She is thirteen years old, very cute—wearing blue jeans, sneakers and a "Dewey Webber Surf Board" T-shirt which hangs to her knees. John seems slightly panicked.

JOHN: Ah, shit,—how old are you?

CAROL: Old enough. How old are you?

JOHN: I'm too old for you.

CAROL: You can't be that old.

JOHN: Listen, listen. I think you better go back and sit with your sister. Hey, ah . . . where are they anyway? They comin' back or somethin'? This is a joke, right? This better be a joke, 'cause I'm not drivin' you around.

CAROL: But you asked me. What's the matter? Am I too ugly? (*on the verge of tears*) Judy doesn't want me with her and now you don't want me with you. Nobody wants me . . . even my mother and father hate me. Everybody hates me.

JOHN: No they don't. I mean, I don't know, maybe they do. But I don't. It's just that you're a little young for me.

CAROL: I am not! If you throw me out I'll scream.

JOHN: OK, OK, just stay cool. There's no need to scream. We'll think of something. (*He looks at her as she wipes her eyes.*) It shouldn't take too long to find your sister again.

Suddenly, a car horn honks next to them. John looks over at the car.

VOICE (*off*): Hey John—you gonna be there tonight?
JOHN: Oh shit! Hey, get down!

John grabs Carol by the neck and pushes her head down onto his lap so she can't be seen. John casually waves to the friend in the car cruising alongside.

Hey, cool . . .

Carol's head is being held down on his lap. She looks up at him.

CAROL: Hey, is this what they call copping a feel?

John jumps, and immediately lets go of her as if burned.

JOHN: NO! Uh uh. N-O. Don't even say that. Jesus . . .

John is beginning to sweat now.

CAROL: What's your name?
JOHN: Mud, if anybody sees you.

CRUISING G STREET—STEVE'S '58 CHEVY

Terry continues to cruise the main drag, slouched low and looking cool in his newly acquired machine. He adjusts his waterfall curl as the Wolfman dedicates a list of songs. He passes a group of guys bullshitting around the raised hood of a souped-up parked car.

Terry cruises alongside two girls in a Ford. He revs the engine to get their attention and once he has it he motions to roll down their window. They flip him the bird instead and he lets them pass.

Terry pulls up to a stop light. The car next to him is a '56 Ford—a good opponent and besides, the kid driving looks younger than Terry.

TERRY: What you got in there, kid?
KID: More than you can handle.

Terry revs his engine. So does the Ford. The tension mounts. The green arrow for the left turn lane flashes on, the car on Terry's other side moves off, and before he can control his reflexes, Terry, too, has shot into the intersection while the light remains red! Terry quickly shifts and returns to the starting position. The other driver is grinning. Terry is flustered and embarrassed. Terry revs the Chevy a couple more times, concentrating intently this time on the right light.

Green! . . . The Ford bolts into the intersection. Terry likewise floors the gas pedal and goes crashing backwards into a large Buick. Terry is stunned for a moment, then realizes he forgot to shift into first. He fumbles to get the car into first gear.

A distinguished looking man comes up to his window after inspecting the damage. Terry tries to escape, but in his panic the engine dies. He struggles to start it.

OLDER MAN: Excuse me, but I think we've had an accident.
TERRY: Well, goddamnit, I won't report you this time, but next time just watch it, will ya?

Terry roars off in a cloud of indignant smoke, leav-

ing the gentleman standing in the street looking dis-mayed. The cars behind him begin to honk their horns and shout crudities.

USED CAR LOT

Terry pulls up in front of a used car lot and jumps out to inspect the damage to Steve's Chevy. He rubs a small scratch on the back fender, but it won't dis-appear. As he spits on it, a slick, baggy-suited car salesman ambles up.

SALESMAN: I'll give you $525 for her on a practically new Corvette . . . and on top of this, I'm going to knock 10% off the low price of this beautiful Vette. I'm talking about only $98 down and $98 a month. Now, how am I able to make you this incredible offer? I'll tell you! I'm forced to move all the sporty cars off the lot as quickly as I can. Boss's orders. He doesn't want 'em. I think it's a mistake, but what can I do?

Terry begins to get worried as the salesman begins to fondle his new Chevy. He becomes frightened as the salesman attempts to drag him over to one of the 'Vettes. Finally Terry breaks away and jumps back into his car and the salesman continues to rave on as Terry drives away.

HIGH SCHOOL GYM—"AT THE HOP"

Herbie and the Heartbeats, wearing their matching red blazers, rock into a raunchy rendition of their masterpiece— .

35

HERBIE AND THE HEARTBEATS: One, two, three, four—
one, two, three, four—

      BAH . . . BAH . . . BAH . . . BAH . . .
      BAH . . . BAH . . . BAH . . . BAH . . .
      BAH . . . BAH . . . BAH . . . BAH . . .
      BAH . . . BAH . . . BAH . . . BAH . . .
      At the hop ! !

*Pulling back from the bandstand, we see the Dewey
High School gym—the basketball nets swung back and
draped with crepe, the lights half-low, the noise high,*

and the waxed floor being polished and pounded by stockinged feet as a seething mob of adolescents join in that ancient rite—The Hop.

A hundred of them are dancing and swaying while the band gyrates on a raised platform. Kids on wooden bleachers watch the whirling and spinning mass of ponytails and ducktails, button-down shirts and mid-calf skirts, cardigan sweaters with little belts in the back.

THE GIRLS' LAVATORY

Laurie stands in front of a mirror in a line of other girls. She brushes her hair, staring rather despondently at herself in the mirror. The girl next to her is Peg Fuller, a cute cheerleader.

PEG: Hey, why are you so depressed? You'll forget him in a week. Listen, after you're elected senior queen you'll have so many boys after your bod——

LAURIE: I don't want to go out with anybody else.

PEG: Laurie, I know it's a drag but you can't—remember what happened to Evelyn Chelnick? When Mike went into the Marines? She had a nervous breakdown and was acting so wacky she got run over by a bus.

LAURIE: I just wish I could go with him or something.
PEG: Laurie, jeez . . . Come on.

BOYS' LAVATORY

We move down a row of sinks at which guys are working as intently on their coiffures as the girls. Ducktails being smoothed; glassy waterfalls being primped; the fronts of crew cuts being waxed to stand stiff.

Steve stands looking at himself, then glances at Eddie Quentin standing next to him, dabbing something on his face.

STEVE: What's that?

Eddie jerks his hand down and hides something.

EDDIE: What's what?

Steve turns and pulls Eddie's hand up.

STEVE: Hey, zit make-up! (*laughing*) Wait till I tell— hey, everybody, Eddie——

EDDIE: Come on, Steve—don't. Just cool it.

He takes his pimple cream back and Steve continues to laugh. He stops slowly and looks at himself again in the mirror. He finds something on his neck, looks around at Eddie.

STEVE (*quietly*): Let me see some of that stuff.

Eddie gives him the tube and Steve dabs it on his neck.

EDDIE: You leave tomorrow?

Steve nods.

You and Laurie engaged yet?
STEVE: No, but we got it worked out. We're still going together but we can date other people.
EDDIE: And screw around—I hear college girls really give out.

Suddenly a voice shouts "One-two—" they turn to see a guy at every toilet hit the flusher on "Three," sending a torrent of water down the pipes. Suddenly, there's a rumbling noise as the pipes break and water gushes over the floor. Panic! Everybody crashes for the doors, laughing and shoving each other.

HIGH SCHOOL GYM

The guys tumble out the lavatory door and abruptly cool it as a dumb-looking paunchy teacher stops and looks them over, rocking on his heels. They escape quietly. Steve and Eddie meet Laurie coming out of the girls' lavatory with Peg. They're watching the dancers as Herbie and his band moan through a slow number—"She's So Fine."

STEVE: Come on.
LAURIE: Come on what?
STEVE: Let's dance.
LAURIE: No thanks.
STEVE: Laurie, I want to dance.
LAURIE: Who's stopping you?

Eddie and Peg are listening and watching. Steve smiles at them like everything's okay. He glares at Laurie.

STEVE (*under his breath*): Laurie, I thought since this was our last night together for 3 months, you might want to dance with me.

LAURIE: How sentimental. You'll be back at Christmas.

STEVE: I want to dance now, not at Christmas.

He takes her arm, which she pulls away.

LAURIE: Get your cooties off me—

Eddie and Peg are watching with great interest. Steve smiles at them again. Then he leans down and whispers something to Laurie.

LAURIE: Go ahead, slug me, scar my face. I wouldn't dance with you if you were the last guy left in this gym.
EDDIE: Uh, Peg, I think we should dance.
PEG: No, this is getting good.
LAURIE: I'll dance with you, Eddie. You don't mind, do you, Peggy?

She takes Eddie by the hand and leaves Steve fuming with Peg.

PEG: Joe College strikes out.

Steve gives her a snide look, then watches Laurie and Eddie laughing, as they join in The Stroll. The whole gym is Strolling in unison, like some strange musical military formation.

HIGH SCHOOL HALLWAY

The Stroll music floats from the gym down the empty hall. Curt walks along with his hands in his pockets. One last trip down the grey, locker-lined corridor. He slows and stops by locker 2127. He smiles a little, then flips the dial of the lock. Once to the right—back to the left—then to the right again. Curt hits the handle. It doesn't open. Changed already. He shrugs and goes off down the hallway.

Curt walks in the background, behind the line of kids clapping as one couple Strolls down between them. Then Curt hears somebody call him.

MR. WOLFE (*off*): Hey—Curtis!

Curt wanders over toward a young teacher, Mr. Wolfe, who is surrounded by a group of admiring (and grade-seeking) girls. Mr. Wolfe wears ivy league clothes and is about twenty-five, not much older than his students.

MR. WOLFE: Curtis, come here. Help me, will you? I'm surrounded.
GIRL: You won't dance? Come on.
MR. WOLFE: No, really, I'd like to, but I can't. I mean, if old Mr. Simpson came in here and saw me dancing with one of you sexy little—excuse me . . . one of you young ladies, he'd have my rear end.
GIRLS: Aahhh.

They all giggle. Mr. Wolfe shrugs at Curt and heads

for a door. Curt follows him and they escape from the girls into the night.

OUTSIDE THE GYM

Curt and Mr. Wolfe come out of the gym. Mr. Wolfe sees a couple of guys skulking around in the shadows, smoking cigarettes and laughing. The music has changed to "See You in September."

MR. WOLFE: Hey, Warren. Come on, gentlemen, back inside. Put 'em out. Let's go.

CURT (*grinning as he pulls out a pack of cigarettes*): Kids . . . Want one?

MR. WOLFE (*taking one from the pack*): All right. Hey, I thought you'd left.

CURT: No, not yet. (*looking for matches*) I have no matches.

Mr. Wolfe takes out a pack of matches and lights both their cigarettes. They walk down a chain-link fence, past dark, venetian-blinded classrooms.

MR. WOLFE: Brother, how do I get stuck with dance supervision? Will you tell me that? . . . You going back East? Boy, I remember the day I went off. Got drunk as hell the night before. Just——

CURT: Blotto.

MR. WOLFE: Blotto. Exactly. Barfed on the train all the next day.

CURT (*grinning*): Cute. Very cute. Where'd you go again?

MR. WOLFE: Middlebury. Vermont. Got a scholarship.

CURT: And only stayed a semester.

MR. WOLFE (*smiling and nodding*): One semester. And after all that, I came back here.

CURT: Why?

MR. WOLFE (*shrugging*): Decided I wasn't the competitive type. I don't know . . . maybe I was scared.

CURT: Well, you know I might find I'm not the competitive type myself.

MR. WOLFE: What do you mean?

CURT: Well, I'm not really sure that I'm going.

MR. WOLFE: Hey, now—don't be stupid. Go. Experience life. Have some fun, Curtis.

Then a voice calls from the shadows.

JANE (*off*): Bill?

They turn and see a girl coming out of a doorway. Mr. Wolfe looks at Jane, one of his students, but doesn't say anything.

JANE: I mean—Mr. Wolfe. Can I speak with you a minute. (*She smiles at Curt.*) Hi, Curt.

CURT: Jane . . .

He looks at Mr. Wolfe, who seems a little embarrassed. Then, Mr. Wolfe sticks out his hand.

MR. WOLFE: Anyway—good luck, Curtis.

Curt shakes his hand.

CURT: Yeah . . . I'll see you. Thanks a lot.

Curt walks back toward the gym. Looking around,

he sees Mr. Wolfe standing in the shadows with the girl, talking intimately. Curt turns away and goes off. Before going back into the gym, Curt stops. He sees a white T-bird parked among a row of cars in the parking lot. He walks—then starts running toward the car. There's a blonde sitting in the front seat making out with some guy.

Curt leans down to the window and is about to say something to his dream girl. But she turns and he sees it's not her. Her boyfriend glares at him like he's some kind of peeping Tom. Curt backs away awkwardly, trying to smile. He leaves.

CRUISING MAIN STREET–'32 DEUCE COUPE

The yellow Ford coupe is gliding down the street—skimming around corners gracefully as the night lights glide up its lacquered hood.

Inside the car, Carol glances at John and smiles. The Wolfman is howling on the radio.

WOLFMAN (*voice over*): A Wolfman exclusive for ya now. The Beach Boys, baby, a brand new group. I predict they gonna go a long way. This is called "Surfin' Safari."

Carol is continuing to jabber on, relating past adventures with her little friends. John is unimpressed.

CAROL: So the next night we found out where they parked and went out with ammunition.
JOHN: Don't you have homework or something to do?
CAROL: No sweat—my mother does it. Anyway, he thought he was had. He started the car and couldn't see through the windshield—and zoomed straight

into the canal—it was a riot.

John smiles sarcastically.

I still got some, so don't try anything.

She takes a pressurized can of shaving cream and squirts his nose. He swipes at the shaving cream on his nose—swerving—A car honks.

JOHN: Hey, watch it will ya! Jesus Christ, thanks a lot. (*looking at her angrily*) Hey, drivin' is a serious business. I ain't havin' no accidents because of you.

Carol sinks into her corner of the car. She sticks her tongue out for a quick moment.

(*catching her look*) Come on, don't give me any grief. I'm warning ya.
CAROL: Spare me, killer.

He stares at her and she shuts up. "Surfin' Safari" is blaring on the radio and she starts twisting with the

music. John turns the radio off.

CAROL: Why'd you do that?

JOHN: I don't like that surfing shit. Rock 'n Roll's been going downhill ever since Buddy Holly died.

CAROL: Don't you think the Beach Boys are boss!

JOHN: You would, you grungy little twerp.

CAROL: Grungy? You big weenie, if I had a boyfriend he'd pound you.

JOHN (*looking in the rear-view mirror*): Sure—ah, shit, Holstein!

She looks around, and sees a police car following them, bubble lights aglow.

CAROL: Good, a cop—I'm going to tell him you tried to rape me.

John pulls the car over and stops.

JOHN: Oh no—No. Hey——

CAROL: It's past curfew. I'm going to tell him how old I am, my parents don't know I'm out and you

tried to rape me. Boy, are you up a creek.

John looks at her.

JOHN: Hey—ah, really—don't say anything.

She looks at him.

CAROL: If you say "I was a dirty bird. Carol's not grungy, she's bitchin'."

The cop is tapping at John's window. John wipes his face.

CAROL: Say it—I'll tell him.
JOHN (*quietly*): I was a dirty bird, Carol's not grungy, she's bitchin'.
CAROL: Okay—I'll think about it.

"The Great Imposter" can be heard on the passing car radios.
John rolls down his window. He looks at the surly cop.

HOLSTEIN: Where you going, Milner?
JOHN: I'm going home—sir.
HOLSTEIN: Where you been, Milner?
JOHN: Ah—at the movies—sir.
HOLSTEIN: Milner, you weren't around the 12th and G streets at about 8:30, were you?
JOHN: No, I was at the movies—like I said—sir.

Holstein looks at him, then steps back, looks at the car. Holstein's only a couple of years older than John, but the uniform separates them by light years.

HOLSTEIN: Uh-huh. Milner, the reason I stopped you was because the light on your license plate is out. (*opening his ticket book*) I'm gonna have to cite you for that. And Milner, the front end of this . . . this . . . this thing you're driving looks a little low.

JOHN: Oh, no sir. It's twelve and a half inches. Regulation size. Now, it's been checked several times. You can check it if you like, sir.

Holstein just glares at him and then leans in close through the window.

HOLSTEIN: Look, Milner.
JOHN: Yes, sir.
HOLSTEIN: You can't fool with the law.

JOHN: Yes, sir.

HOLSTEIN: We know that was you tonight. We have an excellent description of this car. I could run you in right now and I could make it stick. But I'm not gonna do that, Milner, you know why?

John shakes his head no.

Because I want to catch you in the act. And when I do, I'm gonna nail you, but good. Happy Birthday, Milner.

Holstein drops the ticket through the window onto John's lap. He starts back to his patrol car. When he's out of earshot John answers.

JOHN: Thank you—asshole.

CAROL (*looking over at him*): You're a regular J.D.

JOHN: Here, file that under C.S. over there.

Carol takes the ticket and opens the glove compartment.

CAROL: C.S.? What's that stand for?

JOHN: Chicken shit—that's what it is.

CAROL: Oh . . .

She looks amazed as she adds the new ticket to a mess of similar tickets crammed in the glove compartment. The police car pulls by them. John scrowls, then roars his engine and pulls back into the stream of traffic.

Terry is looking and feeling like he's got it made. He downshifts and slows for a red light. A very mean-looking black '55 Chevy—blown, scooped and slicked—pulls up next to him. The driver, Bob Falfa, has a gum-chewing girlfriend sitting almost on top of him. Terry challenges the '55 Chevy by revving his engine.

Bob Falfa doesn't even look over. He revs his engine —which sounds like a cross between a Boeing 707 and a SuperChief. Terry can't believe it. He quits revving his engine—feeling deflated.

Terry looks over at the snotty grin on Falfa's girlfriend's face.

GIRLFRIEND: Ain't he neat?

Terry doesn't say anything and Bob Falfa glares over at him.

FALFA: Hey, you know a guy around here with a piss yellow deuce coupe—supposed to be hot stuff?
TERRY: You mean John Milner?

Falfa nods slowly.

Hey, nobody can beat him, man. He's got the fastest——

FALFA: I ain't nobody, dork. Right?

TERRY: Right . . .

FALFA: Hey, you see this Milner, you tell him I'm lookin' for him, huh? Tell him I aim to blow his ass right off the road.

GIRLFRIEND (*giving another snotty smile*): Ain't he neat?

Terry doesn't say anything. There's another incredible scream as Falfa roars off, leaving Terry to stare through his smoke. Terry accelerates the '58 Chevy—at a prudent speed.

As the radio blares "Almost Grown," Terry glides past the lighted stores slowly, taking in everything with wide eyes from his beautiful new car.

Terry passes a steaming rear-end collision at an intersection where two guys and two girls are all yelling.

Then, suddenly, he spots a girl—walking—alone. His mouth drops open in amazement as he slows to a crawl. Debbie, nineteen, with blonde hair, wearing a blue and white spaghetti-strap dress, strolls along the sidewalk.

Terry roars the powerful engine, but she ignores him. As he passes her, he speeds up.

TERRY: What a babe . . . what a bitchin' babe . . . And Wolfman Baby, she's all mine.

Terry tears around the corner, flashes down the parallel street in record time, hits another corner and starts his approach once more. He quickly whips out his comb, touches up his hair and settles down into a comfortable slouch.

Okay, honey, here I come—James Dean lives!

He hits the clutch, roars the engine a couple more times and then—disaster. Debbie passes behind some rough looking dudes on motorcycles, parked along the curb. One especially vicious biker turns and looks at Terry as he passes.

Terry roars off around the block.

Stay cool, honey—don't let those creeps bug you. Wolfman, please don't let those creeps bug her . . . please.

As Debbie passes the bikers, they hoot, holler and make barnyard noises. From the cat calls, and Debbie's manner it seems obvious that Debbie is a girl a lot of boys have "known."

She has walked clear of the bikers as Terry screeches around the corner again. He pulls up alongside her and again slows to a crawl. They pass each other for awhile, but she doesn't look over.

Hi! (*lowering his voice*) Hello . . . *buenos noches?* Need a lift? Nice night for a walk? Do you know John Milner? Curt Henderson? Sure you wouldn't like a ride somewhere? Did anyone ever tell you that you look just like Connie Stevens?

This stops her and she turns—Terry hits the brakes and the car bounces.

You do! I mean it! Just like Connie Stevens. I met her once.

DEBBIE: For real?

TERRY: Yeah. At a Dick Clark road show.

Debbie starts slowly toward the car.

DEBBIE: You really think I look like her?

TERRY: No shit—excuse me, I mean I'm not just feeding you a line. You look like Connie Stevens. What's your name?

DEBBIE: Debbie. I always thought I looked like Sandra Dee.

TERRY: Oh yeah—well, you look a lot like her too.

DEBBIE: This your car?

TERRY: Yeah. I'm Terry the—they call me Terry the Tiger.

DEBBIE: It's really tough looking.

TERRY: What school do you go to?

DEBBIE: Dewey—can it lay rubber?

TERRY: Oh yeah, it's got a 327 Chevy mill with six Strombergs.

DEBBIE: Wow—bitchin' tuck and roll. I just love the feel of tuck and roll upholstery.

TERRY: You do?

DEBBIE: Yeah.

TERRY: Well, come on in—I'll let you feel it. I mean, you can touch it if you want—(*realizing it's coming out wrong he gets nervous*) I mean the upholstery, you know.

DEBBIE: Okay.

Terry is elated. He climbs out of the car and she slides in the driver's side. Terry climbs back in next to her and slams the door. She's sitting right next to him —like a real date should. Terry gets a little nervous.

59

DEBBIE: Peel out.
TERRY: What?
DEBBIE: Peel out. I love it when guys peel out.

Terry nods, checks his clutch, revs the engine to a high-pitched whine and they're off—
The tires smoke, scream, the car shoots off, fishtailing, nearly hitting a parked car, straightening out . . . and disappears down Main Street.

HIGH SCHOOL GYM—THE HOP

On stage, the band is "taking five." They're looking tough for the girls while the Student Body Secretary is making announcements at the mike.

GIRL: —a great band and they came all the way from Stockton. Let's hear it.

There's applause as the girl continues.

And we want to thank Darby Langdon, who did all these neat decorations.

There's more applause. Standing among the crowd, Steve and Laurie both look angry.

LAURIE: I don't care if you leave this second.
GIRL (*into the mike*): Now the next dance is gonna be a snowball and leading it off is last year's class president Steven Bolander—and this year's head cheerleader, Laurie Henderson.

There's applause, whistles and cheers from the crowd. A blue spotlight floats over the dance floor and

*then lands on Steve and Laurie, who are in the midst
of their argument.*

STEVE: What's wrong with you! You're acting like a
snotty——

*Laurie squints into the spotlight and realizes every-
body's watching them.*

LAURIE: Oh God, come on.
STEVE: Come on what?
LAURIE (*pulling him toward the floor*): Oh, Steven—
please, everybody's watching. Smile or something.

They dance.

*Steve gives a sick smile as she drags him out onto
the floor. A record needle scratches and "Smoke Gets
in Your Eyes" blares out as Steve and Laurie dance
alone in the middle of the floor. The crowd quiets,
getting a little misty about this soon-to-be separated
teenage couple.*

*For their part, Steve and Laurie are still arguing,
whispering in each other's ears.*

LAURIE: You think I care if you go off. You think I'm
going to crack up or something. Are you conceited!
STEVE: Quit—quit pinching—I don't know why I ever
started taking you out in the first place.

*He takes her hand from the tucked-under-the-chin
position and puts it around him, in a bear-hug.*

LAURIE: You take me out? When we first met you
didn't have enough sense to take the garbage out
. . . I asked you out, remember?

STEVE: What do you mean, you asked me out!

LAURIE: Backwards Day—remember? If I had waited for you to ask me—even after that you didn't call me for two weeks.

STEVE: I was busy.

LAURIE: You were scared. Dave Oboler told me. Then when you did ask me out you didn't kiss me for three dates.

STEVE: Well—I was——

LAURIE: Scared—Jim Kaylor told me. I even asked my

father why you hadn't kissed me.

STEVE: Your father—great!

LAURIE: He said he thought you were bright and you'd probably think of kissing me after a while.

He moans.

You didn't, of course. I had to. Remember that picnic?

STEVE: Out at the canyon?

LAURIE: Oh boy! You can't remember anything—the first one, up at the lake. That was the first time you kissed me—I practically had to throw myself at you.

STEVE (*quietly*): I remember.

They continue to dance slowly. Laurie starts to cry, hating herself for it. Steve loosens a minute and looks at her.

STEVE: What's wrong?
LAURIE: Go to hell.

He holds her tighter and they circle the floor, all alone, the crowd watching quietly, the gym echoing with "Smoke Gets in Your Eyes."

THE GYM PARKING LOT

Curt is leaning against a car in the parking lot. He's looking up at the stars and listening to the music floating out from the gym.

WENDY: What are you doin', stealing hub caps?

A pretty, dark-haired girl, Wendy, slides up next to him and leans against the car. There's an awkward pause like that which happens often when two people who used to be close meet after things have changed.

CURT: Well—hey, Wendy.
WENDY: How've you been?
CURT: Fine. Great. How've you been?

A horn honks and Wendy turns to a VW that's idling nearby.

WENDY: I'm coming—wait a sec. (*turning back to Curt*) Bobbie Tucker. She's got her car. Hey, I thought you were going away to school.
CURT: Ah, maybe . . . maybe.
WENDY: Same old Curt. All the time we were going together you never knew what you were doing . . . well, anyway, I gotta go.
CURT: Hey, Wendy—where are you going?
WENDY: Nowhere.
CURT (*smiling at her*): Well, you mind if I come along?
WENDY (*affectionately*): Okay.
CURT: Okay.

They go off toward the VW and climb in.

BACK INSIDE THE GYM

The hop is almost over and the lights have been lowered, conservatively. Steve and Laurie hold each other, hardly moving and he kisses her. Still kissing, they continue to circle slowly—until a short, totally bald teacher comes up and pokes Steve hard in the side.

MR. KROOT: All right, Bolander, break it up. You know the rules. You and your panting girlfriend want to do that you'll have to go someplace else.

He gives them a disgusted look and starts off.

STEVE: Hey, Kroot!

The teacher turns, surprised by the omission of the "Mr."

Why don't you go kiss a duck.

Kroot's beady eyes widen and he comes back.

KROOT: What? What did you say?
STEVE: I said go kiss a duck, marblehead.

Kroot is stunned and people have stopped dancing to watch

KROOT: Bolander—you're suspended. You're—don't even come Monday. You are out!
STEVE (*smiling broadly*): I graduated last semester.

Suddenly everything has changed. Mr. Kroot is furious, but unable to do anything. He finally storms off in a huff. Steve, Laurie and the people watching all laugh.

(*to Laurie*) Get your shoes. Let's go before we get thrown out.

THE GYM PARKING LOT

Steve and Laurie walk toward her Edsel. In the background Wolfman Jack is taking a phone call from someone.

MAN (*voice over*): Hello, Wolfman.
WOLFMAN (*voice over*): Who's this?
MAN: This is Weird Willard.
WOLFMAN: Hold on a minute, let me get my pants off . . . you understand?

Steve opens the door to the car and then turns Laurie and kisses her.

STEVE: Why don't we go out to the canal?
LAURIE (*teasing*): What for?
STEVE: Listen, I can get tough with you too, you know.
LAURIE: Yeah, hard guy.

She kisses him and they get into the car. As they pull out, the Wolfman continues his conversation on the radio.

WOLFMAN (*voice over*): I got 'em down around my knees, man. Wear these tight pants. I can't get 'em . . . All right, I'm gonna do my little dance now, man.

And the Wolfman goes into an insane rain-dance rhythm as we hear "Little Darlin'."

CRUISING MAIN STREET—STEVE'S '58 CHEVY

Terry not only looks cool now, but is cool, singing with the radio, a girl beside him. Hot stuff.

Terry ever so slowly tries to put his arm around her, but by the time he manages it, he has to shift.

They drive by some kids having a car-to-car water pistol war.

TERRY: I go to Dewey too, ya know.

DEBBIE: I never seen ya.

TERRY: I bug out a lot. When I graduate, I'm going to join the Marines.

DEBBIE: They got the best uniforms. But what if there's a war?

TERRY: With the bomb, who's going to start it? We'd all blow up together. Anyway, I'd rather be at the front. I'm like that—rather be where the action is, you know. Once I got in a fight with——

DEBBIE: I love Eddie Burns.

Terry stops, trying to figure out where their conversation went.

TERRY: Eddie Burns—oh, yeah, Eddie Burns. I met him once, too.

DEBBIE: You really think I look like Connie Stevens? I like her—Tuesday Weld is too much of a beatnik, don't you think?

TERRY: Yeah, beatniks are losers.

DEBBIE: Who do you like? I mean, singers and stuff.

Terry slowly maneuvers his arm around her.

TERRY: Ah hell—I like most of the people you like.

DEBBIE (*putting her head on his shoulder*): That's nice —we got a lot in common.

Both of them start singing with the radio. Suddenly she puts her hand on his leg.

DEBBIE: You know what I'd like more than anything in the world right now?

Terry almost does a comic strip "Gulp!"

I'd love a double Chubby Chuck. Isn't that what you'd like more than anything right now?
TERRY (*quietly*): Sure . . .

MEL'S DRIVE-IN

The endless chrome-flashing parade continues. Among the lines of fine cars, Terry is parked in the '58 Chevy next to an order speaker on a metal pole. Terry leans out the car window and orders into the intercom.

TERRY: A double Chubby Chuck, a Mexicali Chili Barb, two orders of French fries——
DEBBIE: And Cherry cokes.

The intercom clicks on and a garbled voice squawks back at him.

INTERCOM: Ark, wark, dork.
TERRY (*pushing the button*): Now wait a minute. What? Huh?
INTERCOM: Ark, wark, dork.
TERRY: Yeah, right. Cool.

As they wait for their order, several guys in various passing cars yell sleezy greetings to Debbie. Suddenly, a rough-looking face, belonging to Vic Lozier, pops in her window.

VIC: Hey, Deb. How's my soft baby?
DEBBIE: Beat it, Vic. I'm not your baby.

Terry nervously pretends not to hear.

VIC: Oh come on, honey. So I never called you back. I've been, you know, busy . . .

DEBBIE: Three weeks . . . besides, it only took one night for me to realize that if brains were dynamite, you couldn't blow your nose.

VIC: Look who's talking. Who's the wimp you're hanging out with now, Einstein?

DEBBIE: Tiger happens to be very intelligent. Unlike you. I know every thing your dirty little mind is thinking . . . (*She looks out the window, down at Vic's pants.*) . . . . . it shows.

TERRY: Hey now—(*his voice cracks*) I mean, hey now, buddy, the lady obviously doesn't——

VIC: Look, creep, you want a knuckle sandwich?

TERRY: Ah, no thanks, I'm waiting for a double Chubby —Chuck . . .

VIC: Then shut your smart ass mouth! I'll call ya, Deb, some night when I'm hard up.

DEBBIE: I won't be home.

Vic makes a kiss-off noise. She lights a match and flicks it at him. He finally leaves.

TERRY: You seem to, ah—know a lot of weird guys.

DEBBIE: That sex fiend is not a friend of mine; he's just horny. That's why I like you, you're different.

TERRY: I am? You really think I'm intelligent?

She moves very close to him and whispers in his ear.

DEBBIE: Yeah. And I'll bet you're smart enough to get us some brew.

TERRY: Brew?

DEBBIE: Yeah.

TERRY: Brew . . . oh—yeah . . . oh, sure . . . (*she kisses him*) Yes! Liquor! This place is too crowded anyway.

Terry backs out and drives off, leaving the approaching car hop standing in an empty parking space.

CAR HOP: What about your double Chubby Chuck, mexicali-chili-barb and—(*looking at the tray*)—two cherry cokes, sir?

CRUISING MAIN STREET—'57 VOLKSWAGEN

We see the white T-bird ahead for just a moment, before it accelerates, passes a car and disappears, as we hear "Peppermint Twist" from the radio.

In the VW, Curt is in the back, shaking the driver's seat, yelling at Bobbie. Wendy is in front next to Bobbie.

CURT: There—don't you see it? Speed up, you're losing her——
BOBBIE: Quit shouting in my ear!
CURT: Cut around him, cut around him.

The little VW swerves and cuts around an old dagoed Dodge, then speeds along the fast lane.

Ahead, we catch a glimpse of the T-bird as it turns a corner.

CURT: There, hang a right—over there!

Bobbie turns, somebody honks, she hits the curb, shifting madly she mis-clutches; the beetle lugs forward; Curt falls back in the seat and Wendy looks at him.

CURT: You lost her!

WENDY: What's wrong with you? You know Bobbie gets nose bleeds when she's upset.

BOBBIE: I do not! You shut up!

CURT: Lost her again. Ah, Wendy, my old love, come back here and console me.

WENDY: Eat your heart out. Who was she anyway?

CURT: I don't know, but I'm going to find out.

BOBBIE: I know her!

There are a few moments of silence as Bobbie lets Curt sweat it out. Finally, Curt breaks.

CURT: Okay, come on, who is she?

BOBBIE: You know Mr. Beeman? He owns Hepcat Jewelers.

CURT: Yeah.

BOBBIE: Well, she's his wife.

CURT: But she was young and beautiful, and cruising 10th Street. You're thinking of someone else.

WENDY: Mr. Beeman's not so old.

CURT: What cruel fate keeps me from my true love? How am I ever going to meet her?

WENDY (*to Bobbie*): Did you know that my ex is going to become a presidential aide? It's supposed to be a secret, but his big ambition in life is to shake hands with President Kennedy. How are you going to accomplish that at J.C.?

CURT: Maybe I've grown up. Maybe I've changed my mind.

WENDY: Maybe you don't think you can do it!

CURT: Maybe you should shut up!

WENDY: Maybe I will . . . and maybe I won't.

CURT: Why don't you move your bod into aft chamber, where we might discuss this in private.

72

BOBBIE (*seeing that Wendy is considering it*): Thanks a lot.

CURT: Come on, Wendy?

She doesn't say anything. They pull up to a stoplight. Wendy looks at the red stoplight and then abruptly gets out of the car and jumps in the back.

WENDY: Well, slide over, I'm not sitting on your lap.

She gets in and the car goes off.

In the back seat, Curt and Wendy are talking softly. He puts his arm around her and she makes a face, but doesn't remove it. Bobbie watches in the rear-view mirror, Curt sees her.

CURT: To the Opera, James.

BOBBIE: Drop dead.

CURT: Unless you want to go to Gallo Dam and have an orgy.

WENDY: You wish.

Curt looks at her and turns her head. He kisses her and puts his arm around her. They neck. The radio plays "Barbara Ann."

The little VW flashes by in the stream of traffic. Bobbie drives, glancing in her rear-view mirror occasionally and also watching the station wagon ahead, in which two pairs of feet are dancing against the back window.

Wendy pulls away from Curt's lips and looks out the window.

WENDY: I've been silly. I'm glad you're going to stay. Maybe we'll have some classes together.

CURT: Maybe.

BOBBIE: (*from the front seat*): Look, there's Kip Pull-man! He's so neat.

Wendy turns and leans forward, laughing. Curt watches her seriously, studying her.

BOBBIE: Do you know Kip?

CURT: Huh? Yeah, I know him.

BOBBIE: Talk to him when we go by.

CURT: What do you want me to say?

BOBBIE: Anything . . . I just want to meet him.

They pull up next to Kip's car and Curt leans forward and yells out Bobbie's window.

CURT: Kip, baby, what's up?

KIP: Henderson, long time no see. Whadaya been doing?

CURT: Not much, just wanted to let you know that Bobbie here is hopelessly in love with you and trembles at the sight of your rippling biceps . . .

Bobbie swerves the car away and turns a corner. She stops on a dime at the curb.

BOBBIE: You creep, fink, son-of-a-bitch——

She turns and starts flailing at Curt with her purse.

CURT: Help, wait! Joke—Joke—Bobbie, remember your nose bleeds!

BOBBIE: Get out—get out of my car—I hate you!

CURT: Excuse me—ouch—Wendy—I got to go now.

Wendy is laughing and Curt climbs over her out of the small car. He gets out and closes the door. Wendy changes seats and looks at him seriously.

WENDY: Curt, I hope I see you at registration. Call me if you want. It was nice seeing you again.
CURT: See ya.

The car pulls off and Curt watches it. Suddenly, he sees something—the T-bird going the other way down the street.

CURT: Oh shit—there!! Wait!

The VW's gone and Curt starts after the T-bird on foot. He runs down the middle of the street, oblivious to the horns honking and the cars swerving to miss him.
We move with Curt as he moves like a broken field runner through the traffic only to finally lose the girl and the Thunderbird and to slow and finally stop, standing on the white line. Cars slow down and kids rubberneck as they go by him.

John is driving and the Wolfman is howling on the radio while Carol is having the time of her life.

WOLFMAN (*voice over*): Went to a dance lookin' for romance. Found Barbara Ann . . . baby . . . Hey, this one is for all you out there watchin' the Submarine Races.

And the radio moans into "Who Wrote The Book of Love." Carol sits with her feet up against the dash. John knocks them off and she scowls at him.

CAROL: I'm so thirsty, I could die. Just a little 10 cent coke to wet my whistle. It won't take a minute, I can drink it in the ——

John suddenly hits the brakes and Carol almost hits the floor. John reaches over and opens the door.

JOHN: Why don't you just get out and get one then! So long, goodbye, hasta lumbago.

She stares at him, shaken, looking sweet and help-
less. He turns and looks at her. A tear rolls down her
cheek slowly. John can't take it.

All right, one coke and then home.

Carol is delighted. She slams the door. John takes
off.

CAROL: Isn't it great, the way I can cry whenever I
want. A lot of people can't do that, but Vicki
showed me how. I bet you can't cry.
JOHN: Don't count on it. I may surprise you any minute now.

MEL'S DRIVE-IN

John cruises around the lot until he finds a space
among the rows of dazzling cars. He pulls in and
leans out to hit the intercom button.

JOHN (*into intercom*): One ten cent coke. Is ice extra? All right, ice.

CAROL: Thanks for nothing.

She looks around, sitting up so maybe some of her friends will see her in John's neat car.

CAROL: Oh rats, I thought some of my friends might be here.

JOHN: Probably a couple of weeks past their bedtime.

CAROL: Wait, there's Dee Dee. I hope she sees me.

JOHN: Oh Shit, Dee Dee!

A long line of cars coast past. Occasionally, someone yells a greeting to John. The car hop brings the coke. Then a couple, Al and Linda, come over. They lean in the window smiling—John prays they don't see Carol.

AL: Hiya, John. Say, do you think if I brought my Mopar by the shop Monday you could spot weld the bumper bracket?

JOHN: Have to be before noon.

AL: Sure. Hey, have you met Linda?

JOHN: No. Hi—ahh, this is my, ahh, cousin, Carol. I'm kinda babysitting tonight.

CAROL: Babysitting! !

She slugs John on the arm. John grabs her arm as she starts to swing again.

JOHN: Jesus—watch it, will yuh? (*smiling at Al*) Been hittin' me all night. Kids will be kids, you know.

She struggles to hit him and spills her coke all over

the car. He pushes her rather roughly against the door.

Watch out—damn it! Look what—why don't you grow up! (*looking at Al again*) We don't get along too well. It's been like this——

CAROL: You spastic creep!

She is about to really cry this time. She jumps out of the car and runs off down the street. John wipes his car out as Al and Linda watch in amazement.

JOHN: We don't get along too well. You know what cousins are like.

AL: Yeah . . . well, I'll see ya on Monday before noon.

John mutters profanities to himself, but his anger subsides after a few moments. He looks back in the direction Carol went. All he can see are two Hell's Angels on choppers rolling in the same direction. He looks a little concerned and starts the coupe.

CRUISING MAIN STREET–'32 YELLOW DEUCE COUPE

John roars along looking for her until he sees her walking angrily along the sidewalk—being followed by a Ford full of guys.

John passes Carol and the Ford and pulls over and stops just ahead of them. Carol stops when she sees John. The Ford also stops and the guys call out to her. She considers the situation a moment, then runs and gets in with John. He pulls off and she grins at him happily.

CAROL: Hi cousin, how's your bod?

79

Terry pulls into the parking lot and stops. He looks up at the flashing liquor store sign and considers his battle plan. "Maybe Baby" by Buddy Holly is playing on the radio.

DEBBIE: Do you have an ID?

TERRY: No . . . hey, but no sweat. What'll it be? Beer, little wine?

DEBBIE: If you could get some Old Harper, I'd give you a French kiss.

TERRY: Old Harper, rrright!

He gives her an OK sign with his fingers and goes over to the store. He starts to enter, then stops and thinks. He sees a man in a business suit approaching, and smiles.

TERRY: Excuse me, sir, while you're in there—I mean, since you're going in anyway, I wonder if—

MAN: Yes, son?

TERRY: Could you—sir—could you give me the time?

MAN (*looking at his watch*): Why sure, it's a quarter to twelve.

TERRY: Great. Quarter to twelve. Thanks a lot.

The man regards him, Terry pretends to start off until the man goes in. Terry pulls himself together as another man approaches, or rather stumbles up, being older, scruffy and, essentially, a bum.

TERRY: Pardon me, sir, but I lost my I.D. in—in a flood and I'd like to get some Old Harper, hard stuff. Would you mind buying a bottle for me?

The bum is still trying to focus on Terry and smiles.

BUM: Why certainly, I lost my wife, too—her name wasn't Idy, though, and it wasn't in a flood—but I know what ya——
TERRY: Thanks, here's enough for a pint.

The old man takes the money and falls into the store. Terry watches and then waves to Debbie in the car that everything is cool.
As he waits for the bum to come back out, the first man in the suit exits. Terry smiles at him again.

TERRY: Hi. Still quarter to twelve.
MAN: Right-o. Night.
TERRY: Night.

The man gets into the car and backs out. Terry goes over to the window of the liquor store and looks to see how the wino's doing with his booze. Terry sees the liquor store owner setting four bottles of cheap wine on the counter.

TERRY (*gesturing through the window from outside*): Hey, no. Not wine. Ssss—hey!

The owner turns and sees Terry waving. Terry ducks out of sight. When he looks back again, Terry sees the old bum is gone! Terry can't believe it. He finally enters the store.

INSIDE THE LIQUOR STORE

Terry tries to look very casual as he sidles up to

the counter. Country-Western music hums over the liquor store hi-fi.

TERRY (*smiling at the owner*): Hi there—ah, say—was there an old man in here a minute ago?
OWNER: Yeah. He went out the back.

Terry is destroyed.

You want something?

Terry looks at the man and the endless rows of liquor behind him.

TERRY: Yeah—ah—let me have a Three Musketeers, ah, and a ball point pen there, a comb, a pint of Old Harper, couple of flashlight batteries and some of this beef jerky.

The owner puts everything into a bag and starts to ring it up.

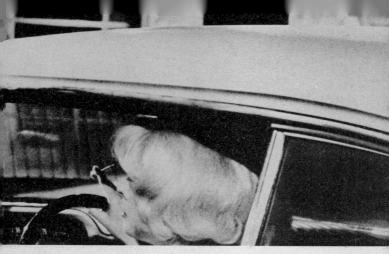

OWNER: Okay, got an I.D. for the liquor?
TERRY: A what? Oh, sure—
   (*feeling his pockets*)
   Oh nuts, I left it—I left it in the car.
OWNER: Sorry, you'll have to get it before——
TERRY: Well, I can't. I also ah, forgot the car.

The owner takes the liquor out of the bag and puts it back on the shelf. Terry stands there. The owner takes the money from him and gives him his change.

OUTSIDE THE LIQUOR STORE

Terry comes back to the Chevy with the bag full of junk. Debbie smiles at him excitedly and scoots over to the window.

DEBBIE: Hey, did ya get it? Ya get it, ya get it?

He hands her the bag.

You got it. You got it!

She goes through the bag and finds a comb and the batteries.

You didn't get it. Why didn't you get it?

TERRY: Ah, well, I needed some things and I thought as long as I was in there—look, Debbie, can you loan me a dollar?

DEBBIE: What? Are you for real? Come on. Girls don't pay. Guys pay.

TERRY: Yeah, well, see—I've only got a fifty and he doesn't have change.

DEBBIE: Well, I can't believe this . . . I really cannot believe this. Here.

She takes the money from a squeeze-open plastic change purse and hands it to him. Terry smiles weakly and goes back to try his luck again at the liquor store.

He stops in front of the door as a young guy with numerous tattoos on his bulging arms approaches the liquor store.

TERRY: Hi—excuse me. I was wondering—could you, ah——

GUY: Buy you a bottle of booze? Yeah, I know. You lost your I.D. What kind do you want?

TERRY (*amazed*): Gee, that's terrific. Ah, just some ah —Old Harper.

He takes Terry's money and enters the store. The clerk hands the man a bottle of Old Harper. Terry waves excitedly to Debbie, lowering his pants a bit. Suddenly, there's a gunshot! Terry whirls to see the young man stuffing cash from the register into his pockets, backing away with a smoking gun. He rushes

out of the store, tossing the bottle to Terry and running off into the night. Suddenly, the owner emerges
from behind the counter, shooting wildly. Terry ducks
and heads for the car with his pint of Old Harper.

AUTO WRECKING YARD

John's '32 deuce coupe crunches to a gravelly stop in front of a dark auto-wrecking yard. John and Carol

get out and climb over the fence. They walk through a valley of twisted, rusting piles of squashed, mashed and crushed automobiles. John sticks his hands into his pockets moodily and stops and looks at one of the burnt-out cars.

JOHN: That's Freddy Benson's Vette . . . he got his head on with some drunk. Never had a chance. Damn good driver, too. What a waste when somebody gets it and it ain't even their fault.

CAROL: Needs a paint job, that's for sure.

John doesn't hear her and walks on.

JOHN: That Vette over there. Walt Hawkins, a real ding-a-ling. Wrapped it around a fig tree out on Mesa Vista with five kids in it. Draggin' with five kids in the car, how dumb can you get? All the ding-a-lings get it sooner or later. Maybe that's why they invented cars. To get rid of the ding-a-lings. Tough when they take someone with them.

CAROL: You never had a wreck though—you told me.

JOHN: I come pretty close a couple of times. Almost rolled once. So far I've been quick enough to stay out of here. The quick and the dead.

CAROL: I bet you're the fastest.

JOHN: I've never been beaten—lot of punks have tried. See that '41 Ford there? Used to be the fastest wheels in the valley. I never got a chance to race old Earl. He got his in '55 in the hairiest crash ever happened around here. He was racing a '54 Chevy, bored and loaded, out on the old Oakdale Highway and every damn kid in town was out there. The Chevy lost its front wheel doing about 85. The idiot had torched the spindles to lower the front end and it snapped right off. He slammed bam into the Ford and then they both of them crashed into a row of cars and all those kids watching! Jesus, eight kids killed including both drivers, looked like a battlefield. Board of Education was so impressed they filmed it. Show it now in Drivers Education, maybe you'll see it. Anyway, since then street racing's gone underground. No spectators, I mean. Too bad.

CAROL: I'd love to see you race.

Carol takes his hand and they walk a bit, until John realizes what he's doing, and drops her hand and pulls away.

JOHN: Come on! None of that.

CAROL: Whadaya mean? I'm the one who's supposed to say that. Whadaya afraid of? I'll keep it above the waist.

JOHN: Funny . . . (*he looks at her for a moment*) Who knows, in a few years—but not now, bunny rabbit.

CAROL: Bunny rabbit! Oh brother, you are such a drip.

She stomps off and gets back into the coupe, quickly rolling up all the windows. John saunters up and finds the door locked.

JOHN: Come on, open the door.

CAROL: If you say "Carol's not a bunny, she's a foxy little tail."

John grins and starts to pull his keys out of his pocket. He stops grinning: Carol grins and dangles his keys inside the car. John leans against the window, closes his eyes, a defeated man.

JOHN (*quietly*): Carol's not a rabbit, she's a foxy little tail.

He hears the button click up and slowly opens the door.

CAROL: You say the cutest things.

John gets into the car.

WOLFMAN (*voice over*): Sneakin' around with the Wolfman, Baby.

The Wolfman's gravelly voice whispers over the airwaves as John and Carol drive out of the shadowy car grave-yard.

WILSON'S APPLIANCE STORE

Curt is sitting on the hood of a parked De Soto watching a row of televisions in the window of an appliance store. Twelve silent images of Ricky Nelson on "Ozzie and Harriet" glow in the dark showroom.

Music from passing cars rises and fades as they cruise behind Curt. The Wolfman can be heard.

WOLFMAN (*voice over*): Oh, this is gonna strike a raw nerve, mama. Here's the Platters.

The Wolfman howls and the Platters wail into the "Great Pretender." Curt sings along, mouthing the words. Then somebody walks in front of Curt.

Curt pays no attention, then senses the presence of another guy. Soon he realizes that he is being surrounded by a group of three hoods. They slink up from all sides wearing car coats with the name **"PHAROAHS"** *embroidered across the back.*

Curt looks them over—they all watch the silent tv's. One of them, without turning, talks to Curt.

JOE: Whadaya doin', creep?
CURT: Me?
JOE: No, I'm talking to the other fifty creeps here. You

know Gil Gonzales?

CURT: Gil Gonzales . . . no.

JOE: Don't know Gil . . . you oughta. You really should.

CURT: Yeah . . . why?

JOE: No reason . . . he's a friend of ours . . . and that's his car you're sitting on.

There's silence. Curt looks uneasy and slides quietly off the De Soto. Curt sticks his hands in his pockets and starts slowly down the sidewalk.

JOE: Hey, where ya goin?

CURT (*turning*): No place. Not going any place.

JOE: Ya must be going someplace—I mean ya left here. Bring him over here, Ants, I want to show him something.

Ants (a tall, ghoulish-looking kid who probably got his name from the scar across his face which has recently been stitched to look like a party of ants marching across his cheek) brings Curt back gently. Joe is bent over looking across the hood of the De Soto.

JOE: Here—bend down, look here. See that? Right across there—see?

CURT: I guess so—yeah.

Joe unbends and lightly punches Curt on the shoulder.

JOE: You scratched it, man. Where do you get off sitting on Gil's car, huh, man?

Joe gives him another charming punch on the shoulder. The others have left the tv's and are watch-

91

ing Curt now, looking puzzled and pained at the
scratch on the car.

CURT: I'm sorry. It's not much of a scratch. I don't
    think he'll even——
JOE: It ain't the size that's in question here. It's the
    principle. Jeez, this is tough . . . what should we do
    with ya?
ANTS: Tie him to the car and drag him.

Curt turns and laughs at Ants' suggestion. He
laughs and laughs until he realizes nobody else is; they
are pondering the suggestion.

CURT: That's funny (*clearing his throat*) Hey, you guys know Toby Juarez? He's a Pharoah, isn't he?

JOE: Toby Juarez. Yeah, sure we know Toby.

CURT: He's a friend of mine.

They all grin and laugh with Curt who feels better.

JOE: Sure, good old Toby. He's a friend of yours. That's cool . . . we all hate his guts.

Curt stops smiling again.

CURT: Oh—well, I don't know him that much anyway.

JOE: We killed him last night.

ANTS: Tied him to the car and dragged him.

Curt looks at them both, praying they're kidding. Joe looks at him, shaking his head.

JOE: This is going to take some thinking. You better come with us maybe. (*putting his arm around Curt*) Go riding with the Pharoahs. . . .

CURT: Well, I don't think I can—I gotta——

JOE: I know just how ya feel.

Joe leads Curt gently but forcibly toward an incredible maroon '51 Merc that's been lowered and chopped so that the windows are like ominous slits and the whole machine has a submarine quality. Joe opens the door and Curt slides into the white fluffy interior. In the small back window, a metal plaque reads **"PHAROAHS."**

The third member of the gang is Carlos, a short little kid about fifteen years old. He appears tougher than the rest with a cigarette dangling from his mouth. Joe heads for the driver's side and Ants and Carlos both go for the front passenger door.

CARLOS: Shotgun!

ANTS: No, I called it!

CARLOS: When?

ANTS: Before we picked you up.

CARLOS: You can't call it for the whole night, man. I got it now. Get in the back.

Carlos gives Ants a hard look and Ants backs down and climbs in the back with Curt. The Pharoahs' Mercury roars out from the curb.

The radio blares "Ain't That a Shame?" as Curt sits in the back seat of the car looking very nervous. He eyes the three hoods cautiously. They are sitting super low, their eyes just visible over the windows.

Then, Curt happens to look around. He does a double take. Through the narrow window he sees the Thunderbird passing in the opposite direction. Curt swivels and watches through the back window as the T-bird disappears around a corner. Then, he shakes his head. Of all the times to be trapped with the Pharoahs.

On the radio the Wolfman is giving a phone operator a bad time and the Pharoahs are chuckling.

As the Wolfman continues on the radio, the cars pass through the night like a metalic ballet. The Pharoahs' Mercury (with Curt aboard) passes Laurie's Edsel . . .

Inside the Edsel, Steve is driving. He puts his arm around Laurie and she leans her head on his shoulder.

As the Edsel cruises by in one direction, John Milner's '32 Ford coupe rumbles by on the other side of the street.

INSIDE THE DEUCE COUPE

Carol is laughing like mad as the Wolfman continues. Even John has to chuckle at the mad D.J.'s raspy patter.

WOLFMAN (*voice over*): Who is this on the Wolfman telephone?

OPERATOR (*voice over*): Hello, Collect . . .

WOLFMAN: Pardon me. Your name is Colette?

OPERATOR: Yes. Collect Call.

WOLFMAN: Your name is Colette Call?

OPERATOR: Sir, this is the Operator.

WOLFMAN: Are you French, Operator?

OPERATOR: This is a collect call for Wolfman Jack.

WOLFMAN: I . . . I love you, Operator.

OPERATOR: Is this Wolfman Jack?

WOLFMAN: Is Floyd there?

OPERATOR: It's for a Wolfman . . . Jack . . .

Carol looks over at John and shakes her head.

CAROL: I just love listening to the Wolfman. My Mom won't let me at home. Because he's a Negro, I think . . . anyway, he's terrific. Do you know that he just broadcasts from a plane that flies around in circles all the time? Do you think that's true?

INSIDE STEVE'S '58 CHEVY

Terry drives on through the wonderful night—a blonde sitting next to him, he's feeling very bitchin'. He and Debbie are also mesmerized by the Wolfman.

WOLFMAN (*voice over*): Floyd, I love you, Floyd. Is

this you, Floyd? I cannot look on thee, love took my
hand . . . and smiling did reply, who made the eyes
but I. Floyd, reach out and touch my soul.

INSIDE THE PHAROAHS' '51 MERCURY

*Even Curt has to laugh at the Wolfman—despite
his situation. Little Carlos sits in the front seat and
looks over at Joe who's driving.*

OPERATOR (*voice over*): Your party's ready, sir.

WOLFMAN: You mean Floyd? Hello, is this Floyd?

VOICE (*over*): Hello, is this Matilda?

WOLFMAN: No, it ain't honey—bye!

CARLOS: You tell her, Wolfman. He's my man. When I
graduate, I'm gonna be a Wolfman. Hey, you know
he broadcasts out of Mexico someplace?

JOE: No, he don't. I seen the station right outside of
town.

CARLOS: That's just a clearing station, man. So he can
fool the cops. He blasts that thing all the way around
the world. It's against the law, man.

In the back seat, Ants nods in agreement.

ANTS: Ah, man—they'll never catch the Wolfman.

*Then Ants' nose starts twitching and he looks over
at Curt suspiciously.*

ANTS: Hey, man, who cut the cheese?

*Curt tries to smile but looks pretty guilty. Then Joe
looks around from the front seat.*

JOE: He who smelt it, dealt it. (*looking at Curt in the back*) Hey, creep, scoot down. Sitting up like that, it wrecks the lines of the car, you know what I mean?

Curt scoots down to a level even with Ants. Ants is staring at him and grinning evilly. Then they hear an incredible roar, and they all turn to see Bob Falfa's black '55 Chevy pass by. Falfa has a new girl with him this time, a lovely redhead.

JOE: There's that badass Chevy again. Look at the snatch he's got with him.
ANTS: Hey, man, he looks like a whimp.

Curt nods and tries to join in.

CURT: Probably is. Whimps gets all the snatch.

Carlos and Ants look at him. Like nobody asked him to open his mouth.

CARLOS: Milner ain't gonna beat that. His time has come. He's getting old. He ain't as fast as he used to be.

INSIDE THE DEUCE COUPE

Milner may not be as fast as he used to be—and having a little teeny-bopper with him isn't helping matters. He looks over at Carol. She's moved closer to him.

JOHN: You got just two seconds to get your ass over in the corner.

CAROL: Don't worry, I won't rape you.

Carol slides back to her side. But as they glide along, Carol watches John. She's moon-eyed and flipped over him. John deftly down-shifts as he approaches a light and then accelerates through the gears with a "race" expertise.

There's a honk and John and Carol look over to see a '60 Cadillac full of girls laughing at them.

GIRL: You got a bitchin' car.

John nods modestly.

In fact, we're gonna give you our special prize for having the neatest car around. You want me to give it to you?

JOHN: If the prize is you, honey, I'm a ready Teddy.

GIRL: Yeah, well get bent turkey.

The girl suddenly launches a water balloon, which John ducks deftly, the tumescent missile catching Carol full in the face. The girls roar off. John cracks up as Carol blinks away the water, not believing what's happened. She wipes her face.

CAROL: All right, very funny. What a chop. Ha ha. Quit
     laughing!!

John tries to control himself, but can't.

Let's catch 'em at the light. Then you jump out and
flatten their tires.
JOHN: Hey, wait a ——
CAROL: Just do what I say!
JOHN: Yezz, bozz. . . .

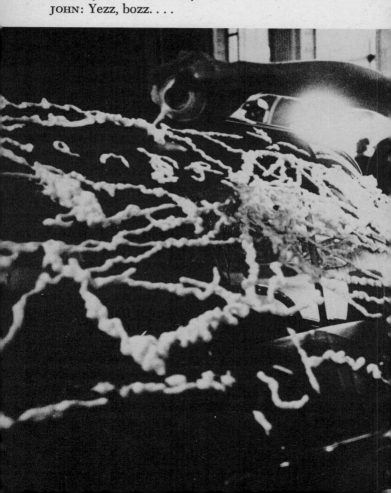

MAIN STREET INTERSECTION

Carol jumps out of the car as John stops the car in the right hand lane next to the Cadillac. As Chuck Berry wails "Johnny B. Goode," they go into action. The girls in the Cadillac recognize John as one of their victims and quickly roll up all windows and lock their doors. John starts pulling the stems from the front tires, sinking the car. Carol starts around the car with shaving cream, spraying all their windows with the

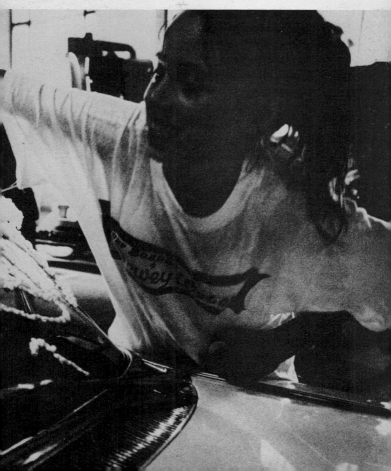

foamy lather.

Carol is having a great time and John is laughing as they continue their guerilla attack. They finish and jump back in the coupe. The light turns green and John takes off, leaving the Cadillac stranded at the intersection, covered with shaving cream. Traffic begins to back up . . . horns begin to honk.

CANAL BANK—STEVE'S '58 CHEVY

The crickets chirp under the full moon. We hear "I Only Have Eyes for You" playing as the Chevy slowly comes to a stop in an isolated spot along the irrigation canal.

Terry gets out of the car, pops the top off two cokes and pours half of them into the canal. He hums, re-filling them with bourbon. He goes back to the car.

TERRY: Tooti-fruiti all ruti . . . It's Super Cola!

He hands her one of the bottles and takes a long drink out of the other. He grabs the steering wheel for support and his eyes begin to water.

TERRY: It's a . . . a little . . . strong, I think.
DEBBIE (*drinking*): It's the living end.

Terry takes a smaller sip this time. . .

TERRY: Yeah, I guess it wasn't mixed.
DEBBIE: Wow, it's pretty tonight. It's a perfect night to go horseback riding—I was going with a guy once who had a horse.

Terry chokes.

TERRY: Oh yeah? I used to have a couple of horses myself.

DEBBIE: Really?

TERRY: I used them for hunting. I do a lot of hunting. Deer mostly, although I got a couple of bear last year. Yep, they were good ponies—hunting ponies. I had to train 'em special, you know.

DEBBIE: Do you still have 'em? We could go for a ride.

TERRY: No, I had to sell 'em. To get these wheels . . . and a jeep. I also have a jeep pick-up, with four-wheel drive. It's got a gun rack. And I use that for hunting mostly.

DEBBIE: Why do you kill little animals? I think that's terrible.

TERRY: Oh, well, yeah, I figure with bears, though, it's me or them. . . . You know, I think you're really neat.

He suddenly grabs at her, putting his arms around her. She's caught off-guard and tries to move away.

DEBBIE: Wait a second.

Terry immediately lets go of her.

TERRY: Oh, jeez, I'm sorry. I don't know what got into me—I didn't mean to—maybe it's the booze or something.

She puts her coke on the floor. She unfastens the chain holding her sweater together and takes it off.

DEBBIE: There—now.

Suddenly, she grabs him and pulls him down on top of herself. She kisses him madly. At first he's surprised,

*but then gets the hang of it. They begin to neck pas-
sionately, encountering many obstacles in the cramped
front seat.*

DEBBIE: Ow—you pinched me.
TERRY: I'm sorry.
DEBBIE: Let me get my head over here—okay, now
you get up——
TERRY: Ow—my leg, my leg. Ow, watch it!
DEBBIE: Ummm, I just love tuck 'n roll upholstery.

*As they roll around, a couple of guys walk by the
car laughing. Terry manages to sit up and watches
them go off into the night.*

TERRY: Geez, it's like Grand Central Station around
here. Why don't we go someplace else.

Debbie pulls him back down on top of her.

DEBBIE: Nah, come on. They won't come back.
TERRY: Wait a minute. I got a blanket in the back.
Why don't we go over into the field?
DEBBIE: All right. Okay.

*They both get out of the car. Terry gets the blanket
out of the trunk. They walk along a path next to the
moonlit canal. Debbie carries their drinks for them.
They left the radio on and Wolfman's voice can be
heard as he takes another call.*

WOLFMAN (*voice over*): Hello.
GIRL (*voice over*): Yeah!
WOLFMAN: How old are you?
GIRL: I'm thirteen, how old are you?
WOLFMAN: I'm only fourteen.

GIRL: Oh, boy, I love you, Wolfman.

SINGERS (*singing over*): "Wolfman Jack."

WOLFMAN: Oh, now we gonna do the weather for all the valleys and the mountain tops. Gonna be hot . . . about 200 degrees in Merced, 400 degrees out in Fresno, and I know we're gonna have about 500 degrees up around the valley somewhere. You got the Wolfman Jack Show.

MINIATURE GOLF COURSE AND ARCADE

As the Silhouettes yip-yip-yip-yip into "Get a Job," we see the mysterious white Thunderbird cruise by and disappear. The Pharoahs' Mercury turns into the parking lot of a miniature golf course.

The doors open and the Pharoahs exit. There's a pause, then Ants reaches into the car and pulls Curt out also. The Pharoahs saunter into the miniature golf compound.

CURT: Hey, terrific, I love miniature golf.

JOE: I hate it.

CURT: Well, I don't play that often really. Ah—what're we doing here then?

JOE: We're outta gas.

CURT: They don't sell gas here.

JOE: No . . . but we're outta money, too. Come on, Carl.

CURT: Curt.

Joe gives Curt a gentle push and they go inside. The golf course is empty, except for a couple of ugly girls putting around in the far corner. Under a trellis, Curt and Joe enter as the Pharoahs fool around with the candy machine, pinball games, "Check Your Weight,"

and "Air Corps Gunner" games, pretending to play
with them.

Joe looks around, whistling again.

JOE: All right, men.

Quickly the Pharoahs go into action, jimmying locks,
pounding coin returns, pulling out plugs, prying open
change boxes and stuffing loose coins into their pockets.

Joe smiles at Curt, who looks sick again, involved
now in robbery.

Ants is sitting in a "Rocket to the Moon" ride,
pounding on it unsuccessfully when suddenly it starts.
Ants starts bouncing up and down looking dumber
than usual. He swears at the Rocket to the Moon
under his breath—suddenly a screen door slams. The
Pharoahs turn.

A man in an undershirt stands by the "Get Your
Balls Here" booth, regarding them warily.

MR. GORDON: What're you punks doing?

The Pharoahs can't think of anything right away.
Ants bounces noisily in the "Rocket to the Moon." The
Pharoahs are all looking to Joe for guidance. Joe for
his part is mumbling.

CURT: Hey, hi. Mr. Gordon, what's up?

The man looks at Curt, surprised.

MR. GORDON: Henderson—Curt Henderson? You with
these punks?

The Pharoahs don't know what's happening yet.
Curt walks over to Mr. Gordon.

CURT: These are my friends. We were just . . .

Mr. Gordon looks skeptical, then Curt smiles at him. Then Mr. Gordon smiles.

MR. GORDON: Jeez, you guys had me scared.

He laughs nervously. The Pharoahs laugh. Everybody's happy.

Hey, you haven't left yet?
CURT: Oh ah—no—no, I'm not—

Mr. Gordon looks puzzled.

I mean, I'm not leaving until tomorrow.
MR. GORDON: Tomorrow. Well, listen, Hank Anderson's inside. Come in and say goodbye. You know, Hank's the one that brought your name up on the floor of

the Moose Hall. You got the check, didn't you?

He leads Curt toward the screen door. Curt looks around at the Pharoahs, who are slowly starting to work again pilfering the machines.

Inside the small office, Curt shakes hands with Hank Anderson, who pats him on the shoulder.

HANK: We are all proud of you, Curt. The Moose Scholarship couldn't have gone to a better boy. And if there's anything else we can do, let us know.

MR. GORDON: Yeah, you'll stay in touch by letter, won't you?

There's a knock at the screen and they turn to see Joe at the screen door.

JOE: Hey, we're all done out here.

MR. GORDON: All done? What—what's he mean?

CURT: Ah, he means, we're all done having loads of fun out here.

MR. GORDON: Oh, well . . .

HANK: Wonderful. You can have all the fun you want. This place is for fun.

CURT: Yes. Yes, it is. Thank you. Thank you both.

MR. GORDON: Good luck now.

HANK: Before I say goodbye, Curt, I want to tell you I hope you'll be taking along with you a little piece of this place.

CURT: I think I have.

HANK: Good. Don't forget us.

CURT: No, I won't forget you and you won't forget me.

MR. GORDON: Okay. 'Bye.

HANK: Good-bye and good luck.

CURT: 'Bye.

JOE: It was nice to meet yuh.

CURT: Right. What he said goes for me, too.

Curt and Joe go out through the arcade toward the Mercury. They start walking faster, anxious to get away. Joe grins at Curt as they climb into the car.

JOE: Yeah, you just might make it as a Pharoah yet, boy.

Back in the office, Hank and Mr. Gordon watch the car pull out.

HANK: Some day he'll make a fine Moose.

THE CANAL BANK

Steve's Chevy sits near the canal. The door is open and the radio blares, while Terry and Debbie are off somewhere in the weeds making out.

Suddenly, a beam from a flashlight plays across the trunk. Feet approach the car as the light beam moves across the interior and stops on the vacated shoes on the front seat.

The light beam continues past the empty bourbon bottle and starts in the direction of the field where Terry and Debbie are lost in the throes of passionate love. As we follow the light into the field we hear footsteps.

As the darkened figure approaches the couple, we see the light go out and catch a gleam of silver in the moonlight as a switchblade springs open!

Terry reacts to the sound.

DEBBIE: What's wrong?
TERRY: I thought I heard something.

She kisses him and he forgets about the noise. The figure retreats back to the Chevy, where another indistinct figure waits.

VOICE (*off*): They're porking in the weeds. No sweat.

Terry and Debbie are resting in the field, listening to the radio in the distance. A car engine is heard starting up and disappearing down the canal bank.

The countryside is very quiet. Only crickets and frogs are heard as Terry begins to drop off asleep. He suddenly jumps with a start.

TERRY: What a minute!
DEBBIE: What?
TERRY: The radio is gone. . . . That means—the car is gone!

He scrambles to the spot where the Chevy once stood.

TERRY: Oh no!!! OH NO!!!

Debbie comes up and watches Terry look heavenward.

Oh God—I'm sorry. But, why the car? You could have struck us with lightning or something—anything—but not the car!

THE CANAL BANK—LAURIE'S '58 EDSEL

Cars are seen here and there in the moonlight along the irrigation canal outside of town. In the cars radios are playing "To the Aisle," laughter can be heard in some, whispering in others.

Laurie's Edsel is parked by the slow-moving water. In the front seat of the car, Steve and Laurie are making out. Laurie leans back against Steve, his arms around her, and they look out the window at the stars. . . .

LAURIE: You know, it doesn't make sense to leave home to look for a home, to give up a life to find a new life, to say goodbye to friends you love just to find new friends.
STEVE: What? Say that again, I didn't ——
LAURIE: That's what Curt said.
STEVE: Oh, figures. (*smiling*) You must've talked his ear off trying to get him to stay.
LAURIE: That's not true. I didn't say anything. Curt just said at dinner tonight he realized there was no big hurry. He thought he should take it easy for a

112

while, go to J.C. and try to figure out what he wants
to do with his life.

STEVE: That sounds logical.

Laurie's expression changes.

LAURIE: You think so?

STEVE: Sure. I think Curt's probably right for Curt. Not
for me though. Laurie, look at me. Now you know
what I want out of life. And it's just not in this town.

LAURIE: I'm not going to the airport tomorrow.

*She looks sullen and he smiles a little. He turns her
around gently and kisses her. They begin to make out,
Laurie seeming a little desperate. Steve pushes her
slowly down on the seat. He moves on top of her and his
hand begins to wander.*

LAURIE: Steve! Don't.

STEVE (*quietly*): It's our last night together for three
months . . . come on.

LAURIE: We've been through this before.

STEVE: I'm going to miss you so much. I need something to remember you by. You don't want me to
forget you.

She closes her eyes, trying not to cry.

LAURIE (*softly*): No . . .

*He starts to move on top of her, kissing her neck.
She struggles for a few moments, then goes limp, not
responding. He pulls away angrily.*

STEVE: What's wrong? You're just lying there.

LAURIE: Well go ahead, you want to.

113

STEVE: Not like that.

LAURIE: If you're not going to remember me for anything else, why don't you go ahead?

STEVE: You want it and you know it. Don't be so damn self-righteous with me. After those things you told me about watching your brother ——

Laurie pulls herself up and away from him.

LAURIE: You're disgusting! Get out of my car! I told you never ——

STEVE: I'm sorry.

LAURIE: Get out! It's not worth it. I don't care if you're leaving—now get out!

She reaches past him and pulls the door handle. The door swings open and she shoves Steve out. Then she starts the engine and drives away, leaving Steve standing there in the darkness. In the distance, he hears the laughter of other couples and the drifting music from their radios.

Terry and Debbie walk slowly along the dark canal. Terry takes a large slug of his bourbon and coke.

DEBBIE: Anyway, the Goat Killer ——
TERRY: Let's talk about something else.
DEBBIE: ——Whenever he strikes, he leaves a bloody goat's head near the victim. Isn't that creepy?

Terry thinks about it and indeed it is. He looks around into the darkness and then takes Debbie's hand.

They thought he went up to Stockton, but two nights ago they found Carlie Johnson and Don White right here by the canal all hacked to pieces and ——
TERRY: Who do you think'll take the regionals this ——
DEBBIE: ——not only were there bloody goats' heads, but he had switched all the parts of their bodies around. You know putting her arms on him and his legs on ——

Terry is slowing and he stops her. He motions for her to shut up and they listen. The wind whines across the flat valley. Ahead there is only darkness, then foot-steps!

TERRY: Wait a second. Did you hear . . . ?
DEBBIE: You think it's the Goat Killer?
TERRY (*whispering*): No! I mean, no. Listen, I'll go for help, you stay here.

Terry has turned and is starting off when she grabs him by his shirt-tail.

DEBBIE: Come on, we'll hide in the field.

She takes Terry's hand and they go off behind some bushes, away from the black water.
Debbie looks through the bushes, squinting.

Maybe if it's the Goat Killer he'll get somebody and we'll see the whole thing.

Terry stands with his eyes closed.

TERRY: I don't want to see the whole thing. Especially if it's us he—oh, why me? I'm going to look lousy with your legs and a goat's head and ——
DEBBIE: Shhh—he's stopped. I can't seem him very— I think he's coming this way.

She edges off to get a better view.

TERRY: Well, as long as he's not—Debbie! Debbie?

She's gone. Terry starts off, taking one step, turns, takes another, turns, takes another. Suddenly Terry hears something behind him. He turns very slowly and looks . . .
A figure is standing right behind him, silhouetted by the moon, its face obscured. Terry jumps about three feet and yells.

STEVE (*off*): Terry!
TERRY: Who, me? Why me?

Terry stops yelling, seeing that it's Steve.

STEVE: Terry.
TERRY: Steve!

Debbie comes back through the bushes and Terry looks at her nervously.

TERRY: Where'd you go anyway?
DEBBIE: Over there.
TERRY: Well, don't go off again. Come on, let's get out of here.

Terry and Debbie start to walk with Steve back toward town. Terry keeps taking pulls from the bottle of bourbon.

STEVE: What're you doing out here? Hey, where's my rod?
TERRY (*choking*): Um, oh, did I introduce you? This is Debbie. Debbie, this is Steve.
DEBBIE: Hello.
STEVE: Hi.
DEBBIE: Hi.

They continue to walk along the dark canal bank.

STEVE: Well, what about my car?
TERRY: Um . . . It's in the garage. I put it in the garage for safe keeping. I mean . . . I mean, I don't want to take any chances with it.
STEVE: Oh, great.
DEBBIE: Yeah. Yeah. It's a good thing too. 'Cause somebody stole our car.
STEVE: Really? That's terrible. What kind was it?
TERRY: Gee, ah, where's Laurie, anyway?
STEVE: I guess we broke up.
TERRY: You broke up? Bull!

Steve just shrugs. The three of them go off into the darkness.

The coupe makes an eccentric swerve as it cruises along the main drag. Inside, Carol is looking at the gear-shift knob that she's taken off the shift arm as they listen to "Do You Want to Dance?"

CAROL: It doesn't look like a gear shift knob.

JOHN: Come on, will ya? Give it back to me.

CAROL: Well, go ahead, cream me. What's wrong, you're a tough guy. Break my arm, see if I care.

JOHN: Forget it.

He ignores her, and finally his silence makes her take a small round knob out of her pocket and put it back on the shifter where it belongs.

CAROL: I was just going to keep it for a little while. You're an ogre, just like my father. He won't let me play records, or stay out late, or anything.

JOHN (*worried*): He ah—doesn't like you to stay out late?

CAROL: No—he's terrible. Once I was at a party that didn't end till late and he called the cops. Can you imagine? It was only a little after midnight and he had the whole police force ——

JOHN: Say, where do you live anyway?

CAROL: Over on Ramona, why? (*she suddenly smiles*) Oh no. Uh uh. You thought I'd tell you where —— not me, not old Carol. The night is young and I'm not hitting the rack until I get a little action.

John sighs, wondering if he'll ever get rid of her. He looks back at something in the rear view mirror. He speeds up and checks the mirror again.

CAROL: What do you keep lookin' at? (*she looks around behind them*) Who's that? You know him? He's following awful close.

JOHN: Grab onto something.

Carol looks scared and grabs onto the dash. John suddenly hits the brakes. The deuce coupe noses down and Bob Falfa's Chevy has to swerve abruptly to avoid a crash.

Falfa pulls the Chevy around and alongside the coupe. He has another new girl with him.

FALFA (*shouting over*): Sorry if I scared ya, man.

JOHN (*looking ahead*): Takes more than that to scare me.

FALFA: Were ya been hiding? Didn't anyone tell ya I been looking for ya?

JOHN: Hey, I can't keep tracka all the punks lookin' for me.

FALFA: They say you're the fastest thing in the Valley. But that can't be your car, man. That must be your mama's car. Hell, I feel embarrassed just getting near ya.

JOHN: Ya should, man—you're drivin' a field car.

FALFA: Field car? What's a Field Car?

JOHN: Field Cars drive through the fields, dropping

cow shit all over the place to make lettuce grow.

FALFA (*laughing*): That's pretty good. Hey, I like that paint job you got. What they call that—sorta a cross between Piss Yellow and Puke Green, ain't it?

JOHN: Yeah, well, your car's so ugly you must have to sneak up on the pumps to get a tank of gas.

FALFA: Well, at least I don't have to move over to let

a funeral go by, man.

Through all the insults, Carol has been cracking up.

CAROL (*shouting*): Your car's uglier than I am.

John and Falfa both look at her and she sits back.

That didn't come out right. . . .

They both stop at a light now. Falfa roars his engine.

FALFA: Come on, boy, prove it. Let's go!
JOHN: Look kid, why don't you go out and win a few races, then come back and see me.
CAROL: Oh, race him, you can beat him.

John gives Carol a very fierce look and she sinks back into her corner.

FALFA: Hey, that's a tough lookin' girl you got with you, man. What're you doin'? Trying to pick up a few extra bucks babysittin'? (*grinning at Carol*) Hey, Doll. Why don't you come on and ride with me—in about ten years?
JOHN: Leave her out of this. This is just between you and me.

Falfa revs his engine again. John thinks a moment, then shifts down into first.
The light changes, and John and Falfa take off, tires screaming. The two cars perfectly in sync, rocket down the block toward the next red light. John starts to slow for the light, Falfa looks over, laughs, and runs the red light. John stops.

CAROL: Wow! He's really fast, isn't he?
JOHN: Yeah. But he's stupid.

CRUISING 10TH STREET–PHAROAHS' '51 MERCURY

Curt is still out riding with the Pharoahs. He seems a little easier with them now, after their successful heist at the miniature golf course. The radio is playing "Party Doll."

CURT: Hey—any of you guys know a blonde in a white T-Bird?
JOE: Yeah, I seen her, what about it?
CURT: I was just wondering who she is.
JOE: She's outa your price range, man. My brother's been with her and he clued me in.
CURT: Price range? You mean she's a——
JOE: Yeah, Thirty Dollar Sheri. Can you believe that? Thirty dollars.
CURT: We must be thinking of different blondes.
CARLOS: Hey man, don't tell Joe what he thinks.
ANTS: Thirty dollars ain't much. I saw ten thousand once. My old man had it in a suitcase. They caught him the next morning though.
CARLOS: Fuzz ahead, watch it.
JOE: Where?
CARLOS: At Jerrie's Cherries. You can just barely see the fender.
ANTS: That's rotten, man. Hiding like that.
CARLOS: That's shitty.
CURT: It's dishonest.

Ants gives him the evil eye. Joe watches the cop car in the used car lot as they pass it.

JOE: We oughta do something. I got an idea. I got a good idea.

MAIN STREET

Steve, Terry and Debbie have made it back into town from the canal. They walk past the closed stores and stop on a busy corner.

STEVE: I think I'm gonna go over to Burger City.
TERRY: Yeah. Yeah. Laurie's probably over there.
STEVE: You really think she's got me worried about where she is, don't you?
TERRY: Well . . .
STEVE: Let me tell you something. I couldn't care less. Want to come along?

DEBBIE: Yeah, I do. I do.

TERRY: No.

STEVE: Make up your minds.

TERRY: No, thanks. U'mm. You know we got to report the car missing.

STEVE: All right. See yuh.

STEVE: Yeah. See yuh.

Steve goes off and Debbie looks at Terry.

DEBBIE: Why can't we go to Burger City?

TERRY: Burger City? Burger City!!? How can you think of hamburgers when somebody stole my car.

She looks hurt and starts off.

ALLEY BEHIND JERRY'S CHERRIES USED-CAR LOT

Curt is getting out of the low-slung Merc and Joe saunters around from the driver's side. He smiles, friendly like—

JOE: Listen, ah—Carl, I——

CURT: Curt.

JOE: Curt.

He nods at Curt, looking cautiously around the dark lot.

Despite you scratching Gil's car, I like you. And I know what you'd like more than anything right now. Like every guy in this town, you got the same secret dream, right?

Curt nods.

Ya want to join the Pharoahs. Huh? You can admit it—you'd like to—but you never dreamed it could be possible, did you?

Curt shakes his head slowly.

Well, tonight, I'm goin' to give you your chance.

Curt hasn't the slightest idea what Joe is talking about. Joe puts his arm around Curt's shoulders and leads him away, explaining what he has to do, while Ants and Carlos grin.

In the middle of the used car lot, a patrol car hides among the autos for sale. Inside the car, Holstein sits with another officer who's dozing. Across Holstein's dark glasses, reflections of the kids' cars cruising by can be seen, as Holstein waits to nab somebody.

Joe approaches the patrol car through the lot. He ducks, carrying a length of metal cable in his hand. Curt wanders behind him. Joe sees him and motions for him to get down.

Get down!

Curt ducks down near Joe.

Okay. Now you got it? I'm stayin' here. You're on your own.

CURT: Wait a minute, wait a minute, Joe. What if he hears me?

JOE: Shhh. Listen. Look at it this way: Now you got three choices. One, you chicken out. In that case, I let Ants tie you to the car and drag you around a little bit. And you don't want that, right?

CURT: No.

JOE: Two, you foul up and Holstein hears you and

126

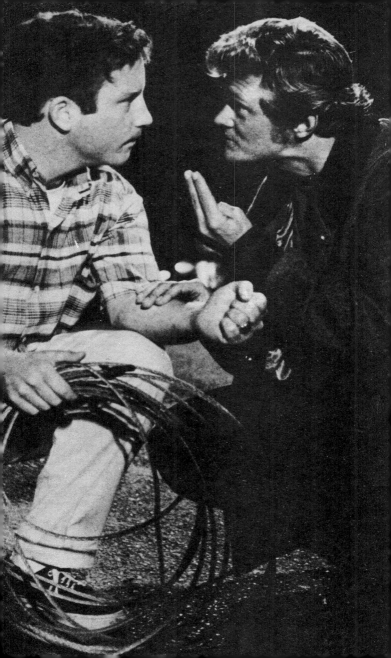

well, ah . . . you don't want that, right?

CURT: No, I don't.

JOE: Three, you are successful and you join the Pharoahs with a carcoat, and the blood initiation and all that, huh?

CURT (*seeing Joe walk away*): Wait—wait a minute. Wait a minute! What blood initiation?

WOLFMAN (*voice over*): Oh, here we go baby! Here's "Come Go With Me."

The policeman waits for a victim. In the background, we see Curt dodging from behind one car to another. Taking cover, Curt makes another break toward a car—and trips and falls.

In the cop car, Holstein thinks he hears something. He opens the door and gets out. Adjusting his billy club, he paces around the used car lot officiously, while Curt hides behind a Falcon and peeks out from behind a fender. He sees Holstein walking back toward the squad car. The cop opens the door again and climbs in. The echoing sound of the calls coming over the police radio blend with the Wolfman's howling as cars pass with their radios blaring.

Curt is inching forward with the cable, toward the squad car. In the background, a slow freight train can be heard starting to move across the valley. Curt ties the cable to a post and then, looking scared, crawls under the police car with the cable.

Underneath the car, Curt inches on his back and then reaches up and attaches the cable to the rear axle of the car.

MAIN STREET

Terry and Debbie are walking across the street,

Terry looks miserable and disconsolate about the loss of the Chevy he possessed for three short hours. Debbie tries to be more positive about the situation.

DEBBIE: Hey, why don't we go get your jeep?
TERRY: What? What are you talking about?
DEBBIE: You know, your jeep. The one you sold the hunting ponies for. The one with the four-wheel drive.

Terry just stares at her morosely. He stops by a parking meter and his head sinks down on top of it.

DEBBIE: Come on, Terry—Terry?

ALLEY BEHIND JERRY'S CHERRIES USED-CAR LOT

Curt and Joe are on the run toward the Merc. Ants and Carlos jump in as they start their getaway.

JOE: Hey, you sure you got enough slack?
CURT: Yeah, yeah. No sweat. Let's get out of here.

MAIN STREET

Joe shifts into high gear and is flying down the main drag. Terry and Debbie look startled as they see the Pharoahs' Mercury roaring by—and Curt leaning out the door, shouting insanely.

CURT: Stand by for Justice!

Terry and Debbie watch the Merc speed suicidally past Jerry's Cherries Used-Car Lot.
Holstein spots them and the driver starts up the

*engine of the squad car. The red lights start flashing
and the siren wails. The patrol car shifts into gear and
leaps forward. Suddenly, there's a horrendous metallic
screech, the patrol car hurtles up and out, airborne
for a moment—then noses down and bounces along
the pavement, sending out sparks as it slides to a stop.*

*The driver is stunned and frozen to the wheel. Hol-
stein manages to remove his dark glasses and looks
back. There, sitting quietly in the middle of the parking
lot, is their trans-axle and two rear wheels.*

*The patrol car sits on the ground at a 20 degree
angle, while its engine whines impotently at top speed.*

*On the radio, the all-seeing Wolfman gives an evil
laugh—*

WOLFMAN (*voice over*): Oh, I can't believe it. Feels so
good 'cause you're sweet sixteen.

*And Johnny Burnette takes his cue and croons into
"You're Sixteen."*

A DARK ROAD OUTSIDE TOWN—DEUCE COUPE

John has glided off the main drag and into a residential area. Everything is dark and quiet as the adult population sleeps through the night. John pulls the coupe to the curb and turns off the engine. He turns out the lights.

Inside the car, there's silence. Only the clock ticking. Carol looks over at John a little nervously.

CAROL: Why are we stopping here?

John looks at her and his arm slides along the back of the seat above her. She notices his arm and the fact that he's moving slowly toward her.

JOHN (*in a husky voice*): Carol . . .
CAROL: What?
JOHN: I—I don't think that I can control myself any longer.
CAROL: You can't?
JOHN: No . . . Carol, I've got to have you . . .
CAROL: Me?

He touches her hair and she slouches back into her corner fearfully.

JOHN: All night you've been sitting there and you've been so sexy and it's been so hot—and I can't wait any more. . . .
CAROL: Well—well, a lot of that's an act, you know. Like . . . like my crying. It was just an act.
JOHN: Well, it's been building up inside of me like a volcano, all night. Maybe if I knew where you lived I could fight it—I could take you home—but since

you won't tell me, and since here we are—I've got
to have you. It's too late——

CAROL: It's not too late! It's never too late! 231 Ramona
—two three one——

JOHN (*smiling*): Two three one——

CAROL: I'll show you! It's easy to find.

*John starts the car engine. Carol looks very relieved.
The yellow deuce coupe roars off down the dark street.*

MEL'S DRIVE-IN

*Steve sits in a booth in the almost empty cafe section
of Burger City. He stirs a coffee and mulls over the
night's events in his mind. A door opens and Budda
Macrae comes in. She watches him a moment, then
takes off her little Bell Boy Cap and gets a cup of
coffee herself.*

Steve looks up as she comes over on her roller skates.

BUDDA: Hi. You mind if I sit down?

STEVE: Hi Budda. No, have a seat.

BUDDA: I got five minutes outa the rat race, and I saw
you all alone. For a change.

*She drinks her coffee and he looks out the window
thinking about something else.*

BUDDA: Where's Laurie?

STEVE: I don't know.

BUDDA: I thought the two of you'd be going strong,
this being your last night and everything——

STEVE: We broke up.

Budda looks surprised.

132

No big deal.

BUDDA: Wow . . . what happened?

STEVE: Nothing. We were out at the canal and . . . we had a fight.

Budda smiles and he looks at her strangely.

What's so funny?

BUDDA: Nothing. Just thinking. A girl like Laurie—I mean, she goes to school and is cute and popular and all, but we're not so different. We know what we want. I've seen her after you for two years now.

STEVE: She's not like that.

BUDDA: Maybe not. She does have a different approach. Hers is "Never surrender," me I lay down my arms at the drop of a hat——

VOICE (*off*): Budda, you got an hour left, let's get on it!

BUDDA (*yelling back*): All right, relax . . . old fart. Listen, I'm off in an hour. If you wanta come over, my girlfriend's gone away for the weekend.

STEVE: I don't know. . . .

Laurie walks up the drive-in and is about to enter when she stops and watches Steve and Budda. She thinks about going in, then hesitates, watching them.

BUDDA: Why don't you? I never got a chance to talk to you. You're leaving tomorrow. Listen, I gave up a long time ago, so it'd be just for fun. No problems.

She smiles at him and he smiles back a little. At the door, Laurie turns away and leaves before Steve sees her.

BUDDA: I'll see ya later then.

She gets up and goes back to the counter on her skates. Steve thinks a moment and gets up also.

STEVE: Budda, Budda wait..

She turns and he comes over to her as she puts back on her little cap.

I gotta get up early and—I just don't think it'd work out.

BUDDA: She's got you so brainwashed—well, hell. Some day I'm gonna win. Don't ya think?

STEVE: Sure.

She smiles briefly, then turns and leaves. Steve watches her go.

MEL'S DRIVE-IN

The drive-in remains a raucous roar: Cars coming in from the hop, from the movies, other cars going out to the canal or back out to cruise. Only the car hops, who have developed a late-hour, harried look, suggest it's nearly closing time.

The Pharoahs arrive. The Mercury swings imperiously into the lot. The radio can be heard as the rumbling engine dies. The Clovers are singing "Love Potion #9."

Curt jumps out of the Mercury elated. The Pharoahs all climb out and circle around him, punching him playfully. Joe holds him while Carlos tickles him and they all laugh.

JOE: Oh mother, it's been a glorious night.

CARLOS: That was the bitchinest thing I ever seen in

134

my whole life.

ANTS: I seen a little kid attacked by pigs once, but this was even better.

JOE: Oh boy, I'll tell you something, that car must've jumped five feet in the air!

Curt nods, feeling pretty good.

You sure you got to go? The night's young.

CURT: Yeah, there's some things I got to do. I still want to find that blonde.

JOE: I think she was an optical delusion, man. Psychology-wise it ain't good to dwell on it. You'll alter your ego or something. Anyway, catch ya tomorrow night.

CURT: Yeah, I guess so.

JOE: Guess so? Man, we don't admit a lot of guys to the Pharoahs. You understand we're going to have to swipe your jacket and all—you gotta make up your mind.

Curt nods, thinking about it. Then he shrugs. He looks at the three Pharoahs as they start to climb back into their maroon chariot.

CURT: Hey—I'll see you guys.

JOE: Sure—listen, remember, Rome wasn't burned in a night.

Joe laughs and Curt nods. He watches the Mercury pull out and then he wanders back across the drive-in toward his little Citroën.

WOLFMAN (*voice over*): My, my, my. You only got five minutes left, if you want to talk to the Wolfman. Gonna make all your dreams come true, baby.

Curt gets into the little car and sits listening to the radio. The neon **MEL'S DRIVE-IN** is reflected across the windshield.

VOICE (*over*): Wolfman . . .

WOLFMAN: Yeah.

VOICE: Would you dedicate a record to keep me and my girlfriend together?

WOLFMAN: Are you separated?

VOICE: Well, see, we're havin' a little problem.

WOLFMAN: I'll bring you right together. Hold on a minute, man. Hi ya, hi ya, hi, hi, hi. Everything's gonna be all right now, man, you understand? Now, let me play the record for you.

As the Wolfman talks on, Curt glances toward the street. He sees the white Thunderbird gliding by. He sits up quickly and tries to start the Citroën—but the machine barely turns over. He keeps trying desperately, but the engine won't catch.

CRUISING G STREET—'58 EDSEL

Laurie drives slowly, alone in the Edsel. On the radio, the Skyliners are lamenting the sad state of things—"Since I Don't Have You." Laurie wipes her eyes, crying with the music. A horn honks. She looks over to see Bob Falfa's car pacing her. He's alone now and grinning at her. Laurie ignores him.

They drive along further. Falfa roars his engine, but she still doesn't give him any attention. He gives up and pulls off.

Laurie thinks a while, pouting. She pulls up alongside Falfa at the next light. He isn't looking at her. She toots her horn and he turns. Laurie motions him to pull over.

Falfa looks surprised. The light changes, and he follows her to the curb. Laurie takes a deep breath and with a determined look, gets out and walks back to his car. She gets in and closes the door. They start off. He looks over and smiles.

FALFA: Hey Hey Hey, baby, what do you say?

LAURIE: Just don't say anything and we'll get along fine.

Falfa is puzzled by the frigidity in the air. He glances at her then back at the road, wondering about this strange chick.

RESIDENTIAL STREET—DEUCE COUPE

The coupe slows in front of a modest California ranch-style home. John stops the car and turns off the engine. He looks over at Carol, who seems lost in thought.

JOHN: This is the first time you've been quiet all night.

CAROL: I had fun. Goodbye.

She sits for a moment, about to say something.

Do you like me?

JOHN: Yeah. I like you. You're all right.

CAROL: But I mean, do you *like* me?

JOHN: I, ah . . . I like you. Okay?

CAROL: Couldn't I have something to remember you by?

John gives in to her sweet gaze. He takes off the gearshift knob, gives it to her, and leans over and gives her a kiss.

JOHN: 'Bye, kid.

CAROL: Gee, thanks. It's just like a ring or something.

JOHN: Yeah.

CAROL: It's like we were going steady. Wait'll I tell Marcia.

JOHN: Wait a minute, now.

CAROL: Wait'll I tell everybody.

JOHN: Don't go overboard with this thing.

CAROL: Well, I'll see you around.

She jumps out of the car and runs up the walk to the house. He watches her stop at the screen door and turn. She gives him a little wave, then goes inside.

John looks over at the empty seat next to him and seems a little sad. He starts the engine and drives off slowly.

WOLFMAN (*voice over*): I haven't cried so much. And the tears and everything, man . . . I leaned down towards the microphone and I almost shorted myself out.

OUTSIDE MEL'S DRIVE-IN

Curt has the front hood up on the beetle-like Citroën and is fooling with the recalcitrant engine. Steve is standing beside him.

CURT: Hold that up.

STEVE (*taking the hood from him*): I've been thinking —maybe you're right. Why should I leave home to find a new home. Why should I leave friends that I love to find new friends?

CURT: Wait a minute, wait a minute. I've heard this already. Aren't you the one who for eight weeks has been telling me you have to leave the nest sometime?

STEVE: I realize that. I realize——

CURT: No—no realizing. You've been telling me all summer that it's time to pull your head out of the sand and take a look at the big, beautiful world out there. Gimme this thing.

STEVE (*letting him close the hood*): I don't know— I——

CURT (*banging the Citroën hood shut*): I feel like a mid-wife.

STEVE: I guess I was wrong. I may have been wrong.

CURT: Wrong nothing. You've been talking about getting out of this town for eight weeks. And now— goddamnit!—you're just—you're just mentally playing with yourself. If you can just relax, we'll talk about it at the airport.

Curt walks around the side of the car and opens the door.

STEVE: Where are you going? It's awfully early in the morning.

139

CURT: I have a dental appointment.

STEVE: Come on, Curt . . .

CURT: Just relax, will ya? I'll see you at the airport.

Curt gets into the car and starts the engine. Steve watches him pull out of the drive-in, then walks off.

ALLEY BEHIND THE "COME ON INN" BAR

A half dozen people are standing around in the parking lot behind the bar. Debbie is sitting on the hood of a car, swinging her legs and chewing gum. The people all seem to be watching something on the ground behind the car. Coughing is heard, then gagging, and the unmistakable sounds of someone being sick.

At the back door of the bar even the cooks are looking and pointing. We hear more coughing and vomiting. A guy slides up on the hood next to Debbie.

GUY: I never seen a guy lose so much. He mustn't have been used to drinking.

DEBBIE: Oh no, he really likes to get drunk. He told me.

An old man looks at his watch and then up at the stars.

OLD MAN: Gettin' late . . . I knew a man once who got this sick. Billy Weber. That was ten years ago. What do you think that was there, that he had for dinner?

More groaning and gagging is heard. An old woman moves close to the old man and he puts his arm around her sentimentally.

140

OLD WOMAN: Staying on his hands and knees like that . . . (*she grins*) He looks like a dog, doesn't he? Looks like old Ginger.

OLD MAN: Sicker than a dog, that's for sure.

The people drift off, leaving Debbie sitting alone on the car. Now, Terry slowly emerges, pulling himself up the hood of the car. His face is white. He lies across the hood trying to catch his breath.

TERRY: Ohh rats, I feel like——(*he notices a car nearby and pushes himself up*) Wait a second . . . hey!

He staggers across the lot toward Steve's Chevy! Debbie slides off the car and follows him.

It's—oh my god—it looks like Steve's car. Look, right here under our—it's my car. *My* car. We found it. Look!

Terry staggers around and looks for the keys. He searches under the front seat and over the visor.

Must've taken the keys with them.

DEBBIE: Maybe we oughta call the police.

TERRY: Never get here in time. I got a better idea. We'll just steal it back. See if you can find some wire around. We only need a foot to hot-wire it . . . okay?

A GAS STATION–DEUCE COUPE

John pulls the coupe out of the garage and wheels up to the pumps of the gas station. An attendant nods, looking at the roaring engine.

ATTENDANT: Took the header plugs off. Expectin' some action?

John looks at him from inside the coupe and nods slowly.

JOHN: Yeah. Think so. There's some punk lookin' for me.
ATTENDANT: Why in the hell do they bother? You've been number one as long as I can remember.
JOHN: Yeah . . . it's been a long time, ain't it? I'll see ya. Thanks.

John drives the car out of the station and screeches down the street.

ALLEY BEHIND THE "COME ON INN" BAR— STEVE'S '58 CHEVY

Terry is fiddling around under the dashboard, trying to hot-wire the Chevy. As the wires connect, the radio comes to life and the Wolfman growls.

WOLFMAN (*voice over*): Who is this on the Wolfman telephone?

There's the sound of a phone ringing, then the unmistakable voice of the Big Bopper answering.

BIG BOPPER (*voice over*): Hellooo, baaaby—

Just then, Terry looks up and sees one large badass looking at him. Terry gets up slowly and sees another big guy standing nearby. The first badass reaches in and grabs Terry by the shirt. He pulls him from the car. Terry is smiling weakly.

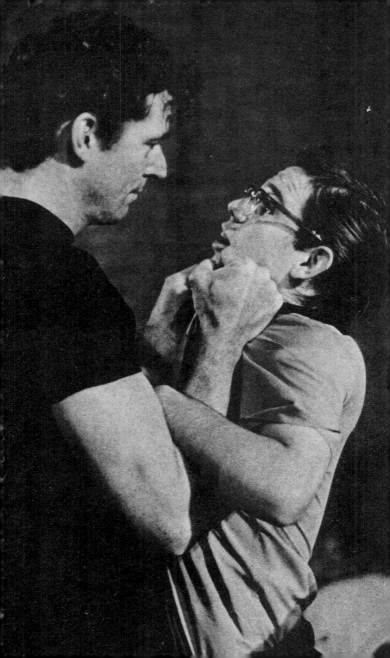

TERRY: Ah, hi—this is my car. What I mean is, somebody stole my—I mean I lost my car and I want to thank you two guys for——

The first badass shoves Terry toward the other badass.

—for returning—I mean finding it. I mean, listen now, listen guys—I've been sick recently, and this kind of activity can really be hard on a guy. Now, easy will you? Easy!

They throw him back and forth and start to rough him up seriously. Debbie is running around helplessly while they pummel Terry. Then, she sees the yellow deuce coupe passing.

John glances out his window and notices the fight behind the Come On Inn. He punches it and wheels into a fast U-turn.

The hoods have quit playing with Terry and are punching him. Terry's still on his feet, mostly because he's drunk and staggering away from a lot of the blows; also, Debbie is screaming and pelting the assailants with her purse.

DEBBIE: Stop it, stop it, stop it! Help! Police! You creeps!

John jumps out of the coupe and runs into the parking lot. He grabs one of the punks and turns him— smashing him in the face. The punk lands on his ass. John starts circling the other.

TERRY: Go, John!
DEBBIE: Hit him!

A good fighter, John lands a couple of blows to the

gut and lands him on his can. Both of them crawl off. Terry is lying nearby, drunk, sick and bloodied. Debbie holds his head in her lap. John goes over and kneels by them.

JOHN: Hey, man, you all right?

TERRY: Yeah. I'll die soon and it'll all be over.

DEBBIE (*looking at John*): Wow—you're just like the Lone Ranger.

JOHN (*eyeing Debbie*): Yeah. Listen, are you with the Toad, or were you with them?

Terry manages to raise his head.

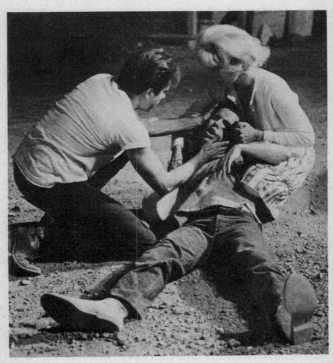

TERRY: You're talking to the woman I love . . .

His head falls back again.

JOHN: What happened, man?

Terry opens his mouth to start to explain, but it's too hard. He can only moan.

MEL'S DRIVE-IN

The drive-in is emptying out finally as the midnight hour approaches and passes. The die-hards and the hard-ups are still wheeling through Mel's looking for remains of any action.

Steve sits inside in a booth. Two gossipy looking girls come in smiling and slide into the booth across from him.

STEVE: Hi, Karen, Judy.
JUDY: Hi, Steve. Have you seen Laurie lately?

Steve shakes his head no.

Well, we have.
STEVE (*already annoyed*): Oh yeah. So what?
JUDY: So nothing. She was just with a really cute guy in a boss car. We wondered who he was.
STEVE: I wouldn't know.
JUDY: We do. His name's Bob Falfa.

The name registers with Steve.
Terry and Debbie pull into the drive-in and park. Terry, his face swelling, groans as he leans toward the intercom.

TERRY: Help . . . I mean, I want two cherry cokes with lots of ice. Never mind, forget the cokes, just bring the ice, pronto.

The intercom repeats his order in a foreign language and suddenly Steve arrives and opens the door.

STEVE: Out! OUT!
TERRY: What??
STEVE: I need the car—now.

Terry gets out and Debbie gets out her side. Steve gets in.

TERRY: What's going on?
STEVE: I'm about to find out.

Steve roars out of the drive-in, leaving Terry and Debbie standing in an empty space.

DEBBIE: I don't believe it! You practically get killed trying to get your car back, then you let him have it.

Terry looks at her, his eye swollen, his lip ballooning, his glasses broken. Finally, he gives up—it's not worth the trouble any longer.

TERRY: It's not my car.
DEBBIE: What?
TERRY: IT IS NOT MY CAR!
DEBBIE: Well, where's your car?

Terry is upset now.

TERRY: I DON'T HAVE A CAR!
DEBBIE: You don't—no car at all. What about your jeep?

Terry shakes his head.

No car . . . well, how am I going to get home?

Just then the car hop approaches with the two cokes on two trays.

CAR HOP: Where's your car? I gotta hook 'em to your car.

Terry shrugs, standing in the empty stall, the carhop with the trays and Debbie watching. There's a low rumbling sound and the girls turn as John's deuce coupe glides into the stall next to them. Terry shuffles toward John's car, a defeated man.
Terry leans against John's car and John looks out the window at him.

JOHN: What's wrong, Toad? You lose the car again?
TERRY (*softly*): No . . . Steve took it.
WOLFMAN (*voice over*): It's a shame, Baby. I'll tell yuh . . . Got to take it easy when you're drivin' that car of yours. You got to cruise easy, baby. Don't be doin' any accidents or anything on me.

And the radio plays "Cryin' in the Chapel."
John smiles and gets out of the car. He goes and opens his hood, making a last-minute check on something. Terry sits down gently on a curb by John. Debbie has been talking with some other boys. Eventually she wanders up slowly and looks at Terry. He looks up at her, then away, disgraced and embarrassed. She sits down by him and they're silent.

DEBBIE: You know, I had a pretty good time tonight.
TERRY: Oh come on, you're just——

DEBBIE: No, no, really, really. I really had a good time.
I mean, you picked me up and we got some hard
stuff and saw a hold-up, and then we went to the
Canal, you got your car stolen, and then I got to
watch you gettin' sick, and then you got in this
really bitchin' fight . . . I really had a good time.

Terry looks at her, starting to regain a little cool.

TERRY: You think so? Yeah—well I guess I have pretty
much fun every night.
DEBBIE: Anyway if you're not doing anything tomorrow
night, why don't you come over?
TERRY: Yeah—well, I might be busy, you know. But
we could—well, I got a little Vespa I just play
around with.
DEBBIE: Really? Why that's almost a motorcycle. And
I just love motorcycles.

TERRY: You do? Well, why didn't you tell me? We
wouldn't have had to go through all that . . . fun.

*He feels his swollen lip and she touches it. Then she
leans over and kisses him.*

DEBBIE: I got to go.
TERRY: Ow.
DEBBIE: Goodnight.
TERRY: See ya.

*She smiles, walks off, swinging her purse. She looks
over her shoulder and smiles. He smiles back.*

The little Citroën bumps along a lonely dirt road, winding its way through dark peach orchards and wizened grape vineyards. Curt watches the deserted landscape when suddenly, the radio increases in volume and he turns it down. Then it begins to roar and distort eerily as the signal becomes more powerful. Then Curt sees it.

He stops the car and gets out. He stands looking at an isolated white frame house hitting in the moonlight. Curt looks up at a spidery radio antenna that rises toward the stars, its black wires humming in the stillness.

Curt starts up the gravel walk to the door. Under the glare of a naked spotlight, he sees a small intercom which plays soft Rock and Roll. He hesitates, then pushes a buzzer. He pushes it again and finally a voice comes over the intercom.

VOICE (*over*): Yeah, who is it?

CURT: It's—I want to talk to the Wolfman.

VOICE: Wolfman ain't here.

CURT: I know, but I got to get in touch with him. I got something to give him before——

VOICE: We don't take no deliveries after eight. Come back tomorrow.

CURT: No, I can't. I want to ask him something that——

VOICE: Dedications by phone is Diamond 75044. Wolfman Top 40 is Box 13, Chula Vista. Wolfman Sweatshirts is Wolf Enterprises, Bakersfield. 'Bye.

CURT: Listen, I got a right to talk to him. I listened to him every night for as long—for twelve years almost. I know him and it's personal and it'll only take a minute and I bet Wolfman would be upset if he knew a friend couldn't get in touch with——

A buzzer interrupts him and the door opens an inch. Curt pushes it open slowly—no one is there. A little scared, he goes inside and closes the door.

INSIDE RADIO STATION

Curt walks slowly down a dark eerie corridor, passing strangely lit rooms with electronic generators, humming dynamos and glassed-off booths filled with flashing electronic apparatus.

Curt goes through this other-worldly maze until he comes to a small, dimly lit control booth. A figure inside is barely visible through the reflections in the double glass windows. The figure turns and walks up to the window. Curt backs off a bit. A face stares at him—long hair greased in a ducktail, a short chin-beard. Then he speaks, his voice filtering strangely through a hidden speaker.

MANAGER: What do you want?

Through the window, Curt can be seen but no sound is heard.

MANAGER: Pull the red switch.
CURT: I'm looking for a girl.
MANAGER: Aren't we all. She ain't here. Come on back to the booth.

Curt walks around through a few more glass doors and ends up in the booth with the manager.
The manager sits down and leans back, turning a fan to blow on his large chest. He's a large, friendly looking man; he wears a Hawaiian shirt. He sucks on a popsicle. Curt stands awkwardly.

MANAGER: Hey, have a popsicle. The ice box just broke down and they're meltin' all over the place. You want one?
CURT: No. Thanks. Listen, ah . . .
MANAGER: Have a popsicle.
CURT: Are you the Wolfman?
MANAGER: No, man. I'm not the Wolfman.

The manager leans forward and picks up a spool of tape. He holds it up as a magician would for audi-

154

ence inspection, then puts it on a machine. A record is about to end. As it does the manager punches some buttons and the record segues into a Wolfman howl and then the distinctive Wolfman voice takes over. The manager adjusts the monitor volume down and sucks his popsicle.

WOLFMAN (*voice over*): Who is this on the Wolfman's telephone?
DIANE (*voice over*): Diane.
WOLFMAN: How're you doin', Diane?
DIANE: All right.

The station manager smiles at Curt, who is watching the tape and blinking lights of the large console.

MANAGER: That's the Wolfman.
CURT: He's on tape. The man is on tape.
WOLFMAN (*voice over*): Do you love me? Say you love me, Diane.
CURT: Well, ah—where does he work? I mean, where is the Wolfman now?
MANAGER: The Wolfman is everywhere.
CURT: But I got to give him this note.
MANAGER (*taking it from Curt*): Here, let me see the note. (*he reads it*) Hell, that's just a dedication. All I gotta do is relay it. And it'll be on the air tomorrow, or Tuesday at the latest.
CURT: No, no. See, this is very important. I may be leaving town tomorrow, and it's very important that I—damn it, that I reach this girl right now.
MANAGER: You don't know whether you're gonna leave town or not?
CURT: Well, I'm supposed to go to college back East tomorrow. And I don't know if I'm gonna go.
MANAGER: Wait a minute. Have a popsicle.

CURT: No, thank you.

MANAGER: Sit down a minute.

Curt sits down, undecided about leaving and upset about not being able to get in touch with the lovely creature he saw earlier that night.

MANAGER: Listen, it's early in the morning. Now, I can't really talk for the Wolfman. But I think if he was here he'd tell you to get your ass in gear. Now, no offense to your home town here, but this place ain't exactly the hub of the universe, if you know what I mean. And well—I'll tell you this much—the Wolfman does come in here now and then, with tapes, to check up on me, you know, and when I hear the stories he got about the places he goes. Hell, here I sit while there's a whole big beautiful world out there, don't ya know. Wolfman comes in last time talking about some exotic jungle country, handing me cigars he says was rolled on the naked thighs of brown beauties. The Wolfman been everywhere and he seen everything. He got so many stories, so many memories. And here I sit sucking popsicles.

Curt looks at him a moment.

CURT: Why don't *you* leave?

MANAGER: Well, I'm no kid anymore. I been here a long time. And the Wolfman—well, the Wolfman gave me my start and he's sorta become my life. I can't leave him now. Gotta be loyal to the Wolfman, you understand.

Curt nods and stands. The manager swivels around and punches some buttons, putting on a commercial.

157

He turns back.

MANAGER: I tell you what. If I can possibly do it to-night, I'll try to relay this dedication and get it on the air for you later on.

CURT: That'd be great. Thanks. Really.

He shakes the manager's hand, then wipes it on his pants.

MANAGER: Sorry, sticky little mothers ain't they? Bye.

CURT: 'Bye.

Curt goes out the door. He starts back out through the maze of windows and electronic machines. Echoing throughout the rooms, the Wolfman's raucous voice follows Curt. The Wolfman howls and Curt turns.

Through the maze of glass, shifting like prisms, he sees the station manager sitting by the mike—howling! Then, he laughs and howls again, starting to sing a song called "Bluebirds on My Dingaling," pounding out the rhythm on the console.

CURT: Wolfman. . . .

He backs away, leaving the Wolfman, who's on his feet now, screaming out the end of the song, dancing by himself in the little glass room, from which his voice radiates out through the night and around the world. . . .

MEL'S DRIVE-IN

John is working under the hood of the deuce coupe when Falfa's Chevy drives into the parking lot. The

158

radio now is blasting "Heart and Soul." Terry moves over toward John's car. John doesn't look up, although he is quite aware of Falfa's entrance.

Falfa slows down in front of John's car and revs his engine again. John looks up—Laurie is in the car with Falfa. She looks determined not to seem as scared as she really is.

TERRY: Hey, John, let me go with you. Come on.

JOHN: Naw, man. I can't take you when I'm racin' somebody.

TERRY: Ah, come on. Just let me go. So I can watch. Or, I'll flag you, okay?

JOHN: All right. Go ahead.

Terry starts to climb into the car. John looks over at Falfa in the rumbling Chevy.

JOHN: Paradise Road.

Falfa grins and gooses the Chevy, peeling out of Mel's Drive-in.

CRUISING MAIN STREET—FALFA'S '55 CHEVY

Falfa looks over at Laurie, who is watching the road nervously.

FALFA: All right now, where's this Paradise Road?

LAURIE: You just follow this street straight out of town. . . . Listen, if you're gonna race John Milner, you can let me out right when we get there.

FALFA: Why don't you shut up, baby? You ain't said one word all night long. What a weird broad. But you're gonna appreciate me soon. You're gonna be hangin' on for mercy, when I get this sucker rollin'.

160

He accelerates the Chevy, shifting up deftly. Laurie looks scared now.

CRUISING 10TH STREET—STEVE'S '58 CHEVY

Steve is cruising along the almost deserted streets looking for Laurie. A T-Roadster pulls up alongside and a guy shouts at Steve.

DALE: You heading out to Paradise Road?
STEVE: Paradise Road, I'm not——
DALE: Some guy named Falfa going up against Milner.
STEVE: John's racing Falfa?
DALE: Yeah. Figured something was up, saw them going out of town real cautious and then——

But Steve is gone. Dale looks surprised as the Chevy roars off toward Paradise Road.

MEL'S DRIVE-IN—PRE-DAWN

Curt pulls into the parking lot just as the neon sign goes out. The last cars are leaving as the drive-in shutters up for the night. Curt stops next to the lighted phone booth and sits in his car, listening to the Wolfman.

WOLFMAN (*voice over*): I got a dedication here that's for a friend of the Wolfman—a special friend of the Wolfman who's leaving town tomorrow and wants me to play the next song for a blonde young lady in a Thunderbird. A white T-Bird, you understand? Now my friend's named Curt and he wants to talk to you out there, baby. So you meet him at Burger City, or phone Diamond 3132. Now he's a friend of mine,

161

you hear, and, little girl, you better call him, or the Wolfman gonna get you.

The Wolfman howls and Curt smiles, leaning his chin on his hand, looking around the dark drive-in, wondering about tomorrow.

PARADISE ROAD—DAWN

John's '32 yellow deuce coupe and Falfa's black '55 Chevy are waiting side by side on a long, straight

country road, their front wheels resting on a weather-beaten starting line. The sky is getting lighter as the radio plays "Green Onions."

There are about six to eight other cars parked off the road to watch the race. Everything is quiet now, only the crickets ignoring the solemnity of the scene, and still singing. Terry jumps out of John's car, John hands him the flashlight and he takes up a position in front of the two cars.

John looks over at Falfa, who's arguing with Laurie.

JOHN: Hey—Laurie, what in the hell are you doing in there? Is she gonna ride with you?

LAURIE: Mind your own business, John.

FALFA: Yeah, she's with me. You worry about yourself, man.

TERRY: Everybody ready?

John settles back in the driver's seat and positions his hand on the gear-shift, which we see is wrapped with rags because of the missing knob.

Both drivers start revving their engines; the tension builds. Terry looks nervous, the engines start to scream and Terry, his hands shaking on the flashlight, manages to flash it on.

Both cars roar off the starting line, tires smoking and screaming. Terry has his hands over his head and is coughing in a cloud of smoke as they pass. John beats Falfa off the line.

Out on the road, as they hit third gear, the cars are almost neck and neck. Inside Falfa's car, Laurie looks scared to death. Falfa looks insane as he tromps it.

John hits fourth at about eighty-five. Falfa does likewise—but starts to fish-tail. Laurie closes her eyes, almost crying—Falfa regains control nervously.

Falfa's engine is winding out incredibly and he begins to get the edge on John. The cars rocket through the dawn light along the flashing white line until suddenly Falfa's car blows a tire, his front wheel slips off and the car shoots off into a tomato field, hits an irrigation ditch and begins flipping over wildly in a horrifying cloud of dust and smoke—

John sees the Chevy leaving the road and screams to a halt, swimming through an unbelievable U-turn and high-tailing it back to the crash site. He is out of the car like a bullet, running across the dirty cloddy field. The crash car is beginning to burn in the engine compartment and John is panicked.

Meanwhile, the spectators have arrived, including Steve, who jumps from his car and is running across the field.

Steve and John arrive at the fire at approximately the same time. They stop, the flames are getting higher, burning up into the trees now. Steve looks around wildly—he sees John and goes at him.

STEVE: You stupid sonofabitch, she was in that car! why did you have——

He takes a couple of swings at John, who finally manages to tackle him around the waist. They both get up looking at the flaming wreckage. Then John moves around the side, crouching, trying to see past the flames—suddenly, he stands and motions to Steve to come over. They both circle the wreck.

Around behind the flaming car Falfa is standing in a state of shock watching the car go up in smoke, while Laurie is circling him, screaming and beating him with her purse.

LAURIE: I said I didn't—you lousy greasy jerk! You coulda killed me—what's wrong with you. You club-foot . . .

She beats at him, crying hysterically. Steve runs over and grabs her, pulling her away. She fights at Steve, too, not knowing what's going on.

LAURIE: No, no, no. Please, don't come near me. No, please. I think I'm gonna be sick. Oh, Steven.
STEVE: Laurie, please.

Standing in the early light, Steve holds her. She throws her arms around him as the crowd develops along the irrigation ditch to watch the flaming car.

LAURIE: Oh, Steven! Oh, Steven, please, don't leave me. Don't leave me, Steven.

STEVE: I won't.

LAURIE: I couldn't bear it.

STEVE: I won't.

LAURIE: Please.

STEVE: Believe me.

John looks at Falfa who's shaking his head, watching the car dissolve.

JOHN: Come on, before she blows.

He pulls him off by the neck of the shirt and when they're a few yards off, Falfa's '55 Chevy does blow—exploding like a small A-bomb, blowing it into Modesto history.

Back on the road, John is heading toward his car, its engine still running, its door open. Terry runs up, trotting alongside John like a puppy.

TERRY: Jeez, did you show him! He'll probably never even get in a car again.

JOHN: He was faster.

TERRY: It was beautiful, John. Just beauti—what?

John stops by the open door of the deuce coupe. Terry stares at him and squints against the rising sun.

JOHN: I was losin', man.

TERRY: What?

JOHN: He had me, man. He was pullin' away from me

just before he crashed.

TERRY: You're crazy.

JOHN: You saw it.

TERRY: No, you creamed him, from right off the line.
The guy never had a chance.

JOHN: Shit, Toad. The man had me. He was beating
me.

TERRY: John, I don't know what you're talking about.
It was the most beautiful thing I've ever seen. That
guy, he might as well—he can get a wheelchair and
roll himself home. Man, you got . . . you got the
bitchinest car in the Valley. You'll always be number
one, John. You're the greatest.

John nods, then looks up at Terry. His face is glow-
ing, his glasses are smashed and his lip still swollen.
John smiles.

JOHN: Look at your glasses, man. (*shaking his head*)
Okay, Toad. We'll take 'em all.

TERRY (*grinning*): Right.

JOHN: We'll take 'em . . . let's get out of here.

John climbs in the car. Terry yawns and shakes his
head.

TERRY: Jesus, what a night.

He climbs in too, and the deuce coupe drives off
slowly as the sun rises over the ploughed fields and on
the radio we hear "Only You."

MEL'S DRIVE-IN—DAWN—CITROËN

Curt sleeps in the little car as the sky grows lighter

over the empty parking lot. The phone is ringing in the booth. It continues to ring. Finally Curt becomes aware of it and opens his eyes. It takes him a moment to remember. Then, panicked, he jumps from the car and rushes to the booth.

CURT: Hello, hello, hello!

A soft sexy female voice is on the other end of the line.

VOICE (*over*): Curt?

CURT: Yeah . . . this is Curt, who is this?

VOICE: Who were you expecting?

CURT: Do you drive a white T-Bird?

VOICE: A white '56. I saw you on Third Street.

CURT: You know me.

VOICE: Of course!

CURT: Who are you? How do you know me?

VOICE: It's not important.

CURT (*excitedly*): It's important to me. You're the most perfect, beautiful creature I've ever seen and I don't know anything about you. Could we meet someplace?

VOICE: I cruise Third Street every night. Maybe I'll see you again tonight.

CURT: No . . . I don't think so.

VOICE: Why?

CURT: I'm leaving . . . in a couple of hours. Where are you from?

VOICE: Curt . . .

CURT: What's your name? At least tell me your name?

VOICE: Goodbye, Curt.

CURT: Wait a second! Wait a second!

But there's a click as she hangs up. Curt looks at the

170

phone a moment, then also hangs up. From the car radio, he hears the Wolfman making kissing noises.

WOLFMAN (*voice over*): Little kiss on your ear. Goodnight, sweetheart. I'll see you later.

And then the Spaniels duh-duh-duh-duh-duh into "Goodnight Sweetheart."

AIRPORT–DAY

A DC-3 prop airliner is warming up its engines as it waits to take off from a small country airport. There aren't too many people around. Just Curt and his friends and family seeing him off. Curt stands with a kindly-looking couple in their fifties. He hugs his mother and shakes hands with his dad.

Then, Curt moves to his friends. He shakes Steve's hand.

STEVE: Good luck.

CURT: Yeah, same to you. And I better see you there next year.

STEVE: Oh yeah, I'll be there.

CURT: Sure.

Curt hugs his sister. Laurie holds on to him for a moment.

CURT: See ya later.

LAURIE: 'Bye 'bye, Curt.

Curt goes to Terry and John.

CURT: So long, guys.

TERRY: Well, stay cool, man.

CURT: Yeah.

TERRY: Ah—don't do anything I wouldn't do.

Curt smiles at Terry, who has a bandage on his forehead. Curt looks at John and they don't seem to know what to say. Finally, John gives Curt a little slap on the cheek.

CURT: I'll see ya, buddy.

JOHN: I know, you probably think you're a big shot, goin' off like this—but you're still a punk.

CURT: Okay, John. So long.

He walks toward the plane and they all wave. He looks around as he goes up the steps carrying a small bag and a portable radio. The stewardess smiles as he passes her. Above the door of the plane it reads **RADAR EQUIPPED.** *Curt looks back again, then goes inside.*

The plane takes off down the runway and then

climbs up into the pale sky.

INSIDE THE PLANE

Curt listens to the radio as the plane takes off. It's playing "Goodnight Sweetheart." As the plane climbs and banks out over the valley, the music fades and the station drifts between static and other stations . . . and then it's gone. Curt turns off the radio and looks out the window.

As the plane banks, through the window Curt sees the white Thunderbird crossing beneath on the small grey ribbon of highway. Curt watches it. Then the plane's shadow ripples over the car and it, too, is gone.

THE BLUE SKY

As the plane flies off against the blue sky we see cameos of Curt and his friends:

JOHN MILNER WAS KILLED
BY A DRUNK DRIVER IN JUNE 1964

TERRY FIELDS WAS REPORTED
MISSING IN ACTION NEAR AN LOC
IN DECEMBER 1965

**STEVE BOLANDER IS AN INSURANCE
AGENT IN MODESTO, CALIFORNIA**

**CURT HENDERSON IS A WRITER
LIVING IN CANADA**

PRODUCTION NOTES

The blast of rock music from an endless stream of cars cruising around the block set the tone for *American Graffiti*. Produced by Francis Ford Coppola and Gary Kurtz, the film is director George Lucas' homage to his teen years.

American Graffiti takes place one hot summer night, sunset to sun-up, in a small California town. The time is 1962, a period of transition for American youth. The kids are wearing ducktails and ponytails and driving fast and flashy cars. We follow four buddies, age seventeen to twenty, who've grown up together, and spent countless hours driving around the neon-lit streets. As we follow these four characters and their girlfriends, the passing cars become a ballet, and cruising a dance in which relationships shift, form and separate by chance. Tonight marks the end of the group, a break from their old lives.

The film's rhythm is set by a radio show and rock

music provided by a final character, disk jockey Wolfman Jack. He's a secret friend to each of them, and each one imagines him differently. The songs represent the sentiments of the characters and also the hopes, dreams and absurd comedies of the beginning of the JFK-New Frontier era—back when the world was simpler and the music sweeter.

American Graffiti was filmed in twenty-nine days, entirely on location in the Bay Area of San Francisco. Much of the area in and around the towns of Petaluma and San Rafael, located about twenty miles north of San Francisco, has resisted the encroachments of developers and has not changed radically since 1962, the year in which the film is set. The task of recreating that era was mostly one of costuming and set decoration. The biggest problem turned out to be hair styles. Girls were reluctant to cut their long tresses, some not having been exposed to a scissors for as long as five years. Boys were uneasy about a greased-back ducktail. Soon, however, everyone was caught up in the spirit of '62 and grease and hair spray were the order of the day.

It was necessary to find about three hundred pre-1962 cars to create the auto-street ballet director George Lucas wanted. Ads were placed in the local papers and soon the production office was inundated with calls from car buffs. Over a thousand people-cars were interviewed before Lucas was satisfied.

Director George Lucas is one of the best known filmmakers to come out of the cinema department of an American university. Following two years at Modesto Junior College where he was a social science major, Lucas joined the Cinema School of the University of Southern California. His only film-related experience at that point was as a still photographer for

racers, but he thought film might be interesting and someone told him it was easy. He made eight short films which won numerous prizes.

Finding professional jobs that he liked unavailable after he graduated, he decided to return to graduate school at U.S.C. where he could make his own films. He became a teaching assistant for a class, giving training to Navy photographers and with half the class assisting him, made a science fiction short called *THX 1138: 4EB*. The film took first place at the National Student Film Festival. He then won a scholarship to Warner Brothers to "observe." He was assigned to *Finian's Rainbow*, directed by Coppola, who has been his mentor ever since.

While working as Coppola's assistant on *The Rain People*, Lucas made a forty-minute film, *Filmmaker*, considered one of the best films about filmmaking. He also expanded *THX 1138* into a full-length screenplay. Warner Brothers agreed to finance and distribute

Director George Lucas, left, and cinematographer Haskell Wexler

the feature and it was released in 1970.

Lucas was born and raised in Modesto, California on a walnut ranch. Cars and drag racing were his primary interests when he was growing up. *American Graffiti* was made on his tenth anniversary of graduation from high school.

Producer Francis Ford Coppola is best known as the director of *The Godfather* which he adapted from the best-selling novel. A unique personality on the American film scene, Coppola is a writer, director, producer and heads his own mini-studio, American Zoetrope, located in San Francisco. His other directorial credits are *Dementia 13, You're A Big Boy Now, The Rain People* (all of which he wrote), and *Finian's Rainbow*. He shared an Oscar with Ed North in 1971 for the screenplay of *Patton*. Most recently he adapted *The Great Gatsby* for Paramount. Coppola produced George Lucas' first film, *THX 1138*.

Coppola has directed theatre and opera in San

Francisco and will soon begin work on a new film which he wrote, *The Conversation*. He will also direct a sequel to *The Godfather*.

Coppola was born in Detroit and raised in New York where his father was a director of musical comedies and played first flute for the NBC Symphony Orchestra under Toscanini. His undergraduate degree in theatre arts is from Hofstra University in Long Island, New York, and his M.F.A. in film from the University of California, Los Angeles. He lives in San Francisco.

Co-producer Gary Kurtz, born in L.A., was associate producer of Universal's *Two-Lane Blacktop* and M-G-M's *Chandler*. He attended the Cinema School of the University of Southern California and began his professional career during college. Kurtz has worked as a cameraman, soundman and editor for Roger Corman and other producers. He has also worked in documentary films, covering the 1964 presidential conventions.

Kurtz met Francis Coppola while both were working on a Corman horror film called *The Terror* and their acquaintance continued through Coppola's *Dementia 13*, for which Kurtz worked on a ten-minute prologue.

Kurtz was the assistant director for two Monte Hellman westerns which began what is sometimes called Hollywood's "New Wave": *Ride in the Whirlwind* and *The Shooting*. He was production supervisor for a film called *The Hostage* before being drafted into the Marines. He spent two years in the Photo Field (similar to the Army's Special Services) as a cameraman, editor and still photographer.

Screenwriters Gloria Katz and Willard Huyck collaborated with George Lucas on *American Graffiti*. Huyck, a graduate of the University of Southern California Cinema School, and Ms. Katz, a graduate of the

University of California, Berkeley, are married, having met at a U.S.C. lecture given by Roger Corman on how to make a low-budget feature. A past editor for the educational division of Universal Pictures, Ms. Katz has co-written with her husband *The Second Coming*, a low-budget horror film directed by Huyck; *Air Conditioned Dream* for Warner Brothers, and *Night Ride Down* for ABC's Movie of the Week. Huyck, an ex-story editor, collaborated on *Devil's Eight* and a Ricky Nelson TV pilot.

Candy Clark (DEBBIE) was a successful model in New York before landing a role in *Fat City*, the only film she has made prior to *American Graffiti*. Born in Oklahoma and raised in Ft. Worth, Texas, Candy went to New York with a one-way ticket and forty dollars in cash. She remembers living at the "Y" on a head of cabbage a day with a cat that was allergic to cat food. Candy now lives in Los Angeles and continues modeling in between film assignments.

Richard Dreyfuss (CURT) was born in Brooklyn, New York and moved with his family to Los Angeles in 1956. He went to school at Beverly Hills High, became an actor and acquired an agent at age fifteen. He has worked on TV in *The Big Valley*; *Room 222*; *Judd For the Defense*; *Mod Squad*; *The Bold Ones*. Theatre credits are *Journey to the Day*; *Incident at Vichy*; *People Need People*; *Enemy, Enemy*; *Major Barbara*. He has appeared in two films, *Hello Down There* and *The Young Runaways*.

Bo Hopkins (JOE) has had two movie roles written for him, something of an achievement for an actor only a few years in the business. Joe the Hood in *American Graffiti* was written with Hopkins in mind, as was the leading role in *The Only Way Home*. He co-starred (with Gary Grimes) in *The Culpepper Cattle Company* and was the sadistic simpleton at the beginning of Sam Peckinpah's *The Wild Bunch*. Hopkins has completed another role in Peckinpah's latest film, *Getaway*, and co-stars opposite Burt Reynolds in *McCloskey*.

Born and raised in Greenwood, South Carolina, Bo still retains a pronounced Southern accent. He has appeared on many television shows as well as in *Thousand Plane Raid*; *Bridge at Remagen* and *Monte Walsh*. He was recently made a member of the West Coast branch of the Actors Studio.

Ronny Howard (STEVE) is best known as Opie, co-star of the Andy Griffith television show for eight years. Ronny has also appeared in *The Wild Country*; *The Courtship of Eddie's Father*; *The Music Man*; *The Journey* and *Village of the Giants*. He has appeared on many television shows, including *The Bold Ones*; *Love American Style*; *Gunsmoke*; *Lassie*; and *F.B.I.* One of the top students in his class at Burroughs High in Burbank, Ronny participated in many school activities, especially basketball. He is now in the Cinema School of the University of Southern California.

Paul Le Mat (JOHN) makes his film debut in *American Graffiti* although he has been acting since high school in San Diego. Drafted into the Army, he spent six months in the Philippines before seeing active duty in Vietnam. Recently he began boxing and expects to turn professional very soon.

Mackenzie Phillips (CAROL) makes her professional debut as the pesky kid sister in *American Graffiti*. She is the daughter of John Phillips of the Mamas and the Papas. A student at Highland Hall, a private school in Northridge, Laurie played the lead in the high school play and was briefly in a rock group, singing and playing the tambourine. She will appear in *Space*, an original musical by her father.

Charlie Martin Smith (TERRY) also comes from a

show business family. His father, Frank Smith, is a well-known animation artist and almost every member of his family, down to uncles and aunts, is involved in some aspect of the entertainment industry. Charlie's first role was in *The Culpepper Cattle Company* and he has since appeared as a juvenile delinquent in *Fuzz*. His television credits include *The Brady Bunch* and *Monte Nash*. Charlie attends California State University at Northridge.

Cindy Williams (LAURIE) recently completed a featured role in *Travels With My Aunt*, starring Maggie Smith. She was also in *Drive, He Said*, and *Gasss* and has appeared on television shows and commercials. One, for Foster Grant Sunglasses, won her an award. Born in California, Cindy moved to Texas for ten years before returning to Los Angeles. She attended Los Angeles City College for two and a half years before turning to acting.

Wolfman Jack, the legendary disc jockey, appears as himself in *American Graffiti*. Wolfman is the personification of "personality radio," the kind of radio that developed in the fifties. The Wolfman came to fame during 1958-66 over XERB, a 250,000-watt Mexican station that was so powerful that a car could travel all the way from New York to L.A. and never lose him.

No one knew who Wolfman was for years. At first it was thought he was black, because of his love for the blues, and his age was put anywhere from thirty to sixty. He himself maintained that mystery until recently when he began making personal appearances and granting interviews. He appeared briefly in a film entitled *Seven Minutes*.

He is of Irish-American descent and was born in Brooklyn, New York. His real name is Bob Smith. He began his radio career at age fifteen, hanging around stations hoping to make himself useful. His personal

style was so strange, and the music he wanted to play so uncommercial that he had to go to Mexico in order to get the freedom he wanted.

At least half a dozen songs have been written about the Wolfman. He is syndicated in 42 foreign countries. Wolfman Jack has a special recording of "Jesus Rock" which features music such as George Harrison's "My Sweet Lord," interspersed with Bible stories told by the Wolfman.

THE CAST

CURT	Richard Dreyfuss
STEVE	Ronny Howard
JOHN	Paul Le Mat
TERRY	Charlie Martin Smith
LAURIE	Cindy Williams
DEBBIE	Candy Clark
CAROL	Mackenzie Phillips
DISC JOCKEY	Wolfman Jack
BOB FALFA	Harrison Ford
THE PHAROAHS (HOODS): JOE	Bo Hopkins
CARLOS	Manuel Padilla, Jr.
ANTS	Beau Gentry

At The Sock Hop

HERBY & THE HEARTBEATS	Flash Cadillac and the Continental Kids
PEG	Kathy Quinlan
EDDIE	Tim Crowley
MR. WOLFE (TEACHER)	Terry McGovern
GIRL	Jan Wilson
JANE	Kay Ann Kemper
ANNOUNCER	Caprice Schmidt

At The Drive In (Mel's Burger City)

BUDDA (CARHOP)	Jane Bellan
VIC	Joe Spano
AL	Chris Pray
JUDY	Susan Richardson
CARHOP #2	Donna Wehr

On The Streets With John

HOLSTEIN (POLICEMAN)	Jim Bohan
JEFF PAZZUTO	Ron Vincent
FERBER	Fred Ross
GIRL IN STUDEBAKER	Jody Carlson
BALLOON GIRL	Cam Whitman
GAS STATION ATTENDANT	John Bracci

On The Streets with Curt

WENDY	Debbie Celiz
BOBBIE	Lynne Marie Stewart
KIP PULLMAN	Ed Greenberg
BLONDE IN T-BIRD	Suzanne Somers

On The Streets with Terry

BOZO	Gordon Analla
GIRL IN DODGE	Lisa Herman

185

FALFA'S GIRL	Debralee Scott
MAN AT ACCIDENT	Charles Dorsett
KID AT ACCIDENT	Stephen Knox

On The Streets With Steve
| DALE | Bob Pasaak |

At The Liquor Store
MAN	Joseph Miksak
BUM	George Meyer
CLERK	William Niven
THIEF	James Cranna

In The Alley
MAN	Del Close
OLD MAN	Charlie Murphy
OLD WOMAN	Jan Dunn
BADASS #1	Johnny Weissmuller, Jr.

At The Amusement Arcade
| MR. GORDON | Scott Beach |
| HANK | Al Nalbandian |

THE CREDITS

Produced by	Francis Ford Coppola
Co-Produced by	Gary Kurtz
Directed by	George Lucas
Written by	George Lucas,
	Gloria Katz and Willard Huyck
Visual Consultant (Supervising Cameraman)	Haskell Wexler
Film Editors	Verna Fields
	Marcia Lucas
Sound Montage & Re-recording	Walter Murch
Assistant to the Producer	Beverly Walker
Design Consultant	Al Locatelli
Casting	Fred Roos and Mike Fenton
Directors of Photography	Ron Eveslage and
(Operating Cameramen)	Jan D'Alquen
Art Director	Dennis Clark
Costume Designer	Aggie Guerard Rodgers
Production Manager	James Hogan
1st Assistant Director	Ned Kopp
2nd Assistant Director	Charles Myers
Production Associates	Nancy Giebink and Jim Bloom
Choreographer	Toni Basil
Dialogue Coach	Gino Havens
Gaffer	William Maley

186

Key Grip	Ken Phelps
Production Sound	Arthur Rochester
Set Decorator	Douglas Freeman
Property Master	Douglas Von Koss
Key Hair Stylists	Gerry Leetch and Betty Iverson
Script Supervisor	Christina Crowley
Transportation Supervisor	Henry Travers
Sound Editing	James Nelson
Music Coordinator	Karin Green
Titles & Optical Effects	Universal Title

Filmed in Marin and Sonoma counties, California, and completed at American Zoetrope Studios, San Francisco.

M.P.A.A. Rating: PG

Running Time: 110 Minutes

MUSIC

Recorded for the film and produced by Kim Fowley:

"At the Hop"	Flash Cadillac and
"She's So Fine"	The Continental Kids

Courtesy of Roulette Records:

"A Thousand Miles Away"	The Heartbeats
"Barbara Anne"	The Regents
"Fannie Mae"	Buster Brown
"Gee"	The Crows
"Heart and Soul"	The Cleftones
"I Only Have Eyes for You"	The Flamingos
"Party Doll"	Buddy Knox
"Peppermint Twist"	Joey Dee and
	The Starlighters
"See You in September"	The Tempos
"Why Do Fools Fall in Love"	Frankie Lymon
"Ya Ya"	Lee Dorsey

Courtesy of Mercury Records:

"Chantilly Lace"	The Big Bopper
"The Great Pretender"	
"Only You"	
"Smoke Gets in Your Eyes"	The Platters
"Little Darlin' "	
"The Stroll"	The Diamonds

Courtesy of Chess/Janus division of GRT Corporation:

"Almost Grown"	
"Johnnie B. Goode"	Chuck Berry
"Book of Love"	The Monotones
"Goodnight Sweetheart"	The Spaniels

Courtesy of United Artists Records:
"Ain't That a Shame"   Fats Domino
"The Great Imposter"   The Fleetwoods
"Love Potion #9"   The Clovers
"You're Sixteen"   Johnny Burnette

Courtesy of Decca Records:
"Maybe Baby"
"That'll Be the Day"   Buddy Holly
"Rock Around the Clock"   Bill Haley and
                              His Comets

Courtesy of Capitol Records:
"All Summer Long"
"You're Sixteen"   The Beach Boys

Courtesy of Bell Records:
"Get a Job"   The Silhouettes
"To the Aisle"   The Five Satins

Courtesy of Sue-Ellen Productions:
"Crying in the Chapel"   Sonny Till and
                              The Orioles
"Do You Want to Dance?"   Bobby Freeman

Courtesy of Atlantic Records:
"Green Onions"   Booker T and
                              The MG's

Courtesy of Embee Productions:
"Runaway"   Del Shannon

Courtesy of MGM Records, Inc.:
"Teen Angel"   Mark Dinning

Courtesy of Original Sound Record Co., Inc.:
"Since I Don't Have You"   The Skyliners

Courtesy of Famous Music, Inc.:
"Come Go With Me"   The Del Vikings

Courtesy of Post Records:
"Sixteen Candles"   The Crests

DEWEY HIGH SCHOOL

YEAR BOOK HONOR ROLL

Hang Loose! your ol' buddy, Big John '60

JOHN MILNER '60
Auto Mechanic

Roses are Red Violets are Blue Tulips are Yellow Carol

CAROL MORRISON '65
Art

Hey! Hey, don't forget to be bad and take me with you! Falfa

BOB FALFA '60
Agriculture

"Rock-a-hot Shot" Curt

CURTIS HENDERSON '62
Science

To a real swell kid Have a nice summer. Always, Laurie

LAURIE HENDERSON '63
History
Head Cheer Leader

To one of the Best People I'll ever know! LUCK, Steve

STEVE BOLANDER '62
English
Class President

Good Luck... from a hot cat to a cool jewel Toad '63 (I hope!)

TERRY "TOAD" FIELDS '63
Business

XOXOXOXO Love, Deb

DEBBIE MEDWAY '61
Home Economics

How's your Boogaloo?

WOLFMAN JACK '51
Finger Popping